HISTORY 1CC3: EMPIRES AND PEOPLE

Fall 2014; Lectures Tuesday, 9:30-10:20; Friday, 9:30-10:20. All lectures are in BSB 147. Tutorials are as specified on your timetable. There are nine tutorial meetings.

Office Hours: Wednesday, 9:00-11:00; Friday, 2:00-3:00.

Instructor: John Weaver (jweaver@mcmaster.ca)

Office: 630 Chester New Hall

COURSE OBJECTIVES

This course emphasizes the importance of diligence, serious reading practices, and good writing. These foundation skills, essential for rewarding experiences at university and beyond, are stressed in course assignments. In the tutorials and on the written assessments of your papers, a tutor will assist with writing advice.

Through the lectures and readings, I aim to promote curiosity about many civilizations and to guide you in that pursuit by examining the history of empires. Empires have been commonplace and widespread. Lectures and readings explain the forces that assembled empires and brought them into violent or uneasy contact with one another. The lectures concentrate first on Eurasia but then follow European sea powers to Africa, America, Asia, the Pacific Islands, and Africa again.

To manage a course that covers more than a millennium, particular empires and organizing themes have been selected. I will call attention to patterns and differences among empires as they dealt with borderlands, control of trade, diverse subject peoples, and leadership succession. The subject material should encourage thinking about connections between past and present. For example, the lectures and required readings explain how the world became more or less integrated by 1900 partly through empires. They left their imprints on distant parts of the world through Diasporas, the movement of religious beliefs and secular ideas, resource extraction, trade linkages, control of chokepoints in trade, and the movement of plants, animals, and diseases. The legacies of exploitation and oppression plus the eruption of recent global tensions related to the legacies of empires will all be mentioned.

COURSE STRUCTURE

There will be two lectures a week and nine tutorials across the term. Please read the agenda and lecture topics section near the end of this syllabus for details. Each student will be assigned to a tutorial group and will be expected to remain in that group; changes in tutorial must be authorized by the departmental administrator for this course Mrs. Lobban. Students will not be marked on participation in tutorials, but will be required at the start of several tutorials to submit written assignments. The final examination will test all course material; therefore, attendance at tutorials will be helpful.

DETERMINATION OF FINAL MARK

Longer reports – 15% each (total 45%)

Report on Crosby- 15%

Report on Brook - 15%

Report on Weaver - 15%

Short Reports - 5% each (total 10%)

Jared Diamond, "Collision at Cajamarca" and "Hemispheres Colliding" (book chapters from *Guns, Germs, and Steel* and reproduced in the courseware). -5%

Peter Perdue, "Writing Histories" and part of "State Building in Europe and Asia" (book chapters from *China Marches West: The Qing Conquest of Central Eurasia* and reproduced in the courseware). - 5%

Library Test - 5%. Earning this 5% is easy. It is an all or nothing requirement. If you achieve a minimum of 80% on the test you will receive the full 5%. You may take the test as many times as you wish during the time that the test is available on-line through Avenue to Learn. The exact dates will be announced in class.

Final Exam - 40%

All written work, except the final examination, will be graded on the basis of 50% for ideas and analysis and 50% for style and organization. Only printed copies of the reports and assignments will be accepted; no e-mail attachments will be read. Along with name and student number students must state the tutorial number on the cover of each written assignment. Thank you.

Assignments submitted late will receive a mark of zero (see FAQ # 7).

E-MAIL

The Faculty of Humanities requires that all email communication sent from students to instructors (including TAs), and from students to staff, must originate from the student's own McMaster University email account. **Instructors will delete emails that do not originate from a McMaster email account.**

REQUIRED READINGS

For final exam purposes, you will be responsible for the articles and chapters of books collected in the custom courseware package, and for the contents of the following books:

Mary Lynn Rampolla, *A Pocket Guide to Writing History.* This book is required for the first tutorial and can serve as a useful guide for writing in this course and others in History.

Alfred Crosby, *Ecological Imperialism.*

Timothy Brook, *Vermeer's Hat.*

John Weaver, *The Great Land Rush.*

Courseware readings for 1CC3 (2014 edition).

OPTIONAL BOOK

David R. Ringrose, *Expansion and Global Interaction, 1200-1700.*

BOOK ASSIGNMENTS:

MANDATORY QUESTIONS, INSTRUCTIONS, AND WHEN TO SUBMIT

In all cases cite page references in footnotes or endnotes. Use full citation information in the first citation and the author and page number only thereafter. For example, in first citation state Alfred Crosby, *Ecological Imperialism* (Cambridge: Cambridge University Press, 1986); in subsequent ones, Crosby, 145. See FAQ # 11.

Crosby (700 words) Due in the tutorial of the **fourth week.**

1. Students with student numbers ending in 1, 2, and 3: How significant is chance or accident in Crosby's account of the spread of biota (people, plants, and animals)? Cite examples from across the book.

2. Students with student numbers ending in 4, 5, and 6: What examples does Crosby use to make the point that Eurasian plants and animals have not always and everywhere totally overwhelmed indigenous plants and animals?

3. Students with student numbers ending in 7, 8, 9, and 0: In what ways does Crosby's history of the Spanish invasion and exploitation of the Canary Islands prepare the way for his account of the spread of European empires and biota?

Brook (700 words) Due in the tutorial of the **seventh week.**

1. For students with student numbers ending in 1, 2, 3: Explain why Timothy Brook considers the seventeenth century "the dawn of the global world."

2. For students with student numbers ending in 4, 5, 6, 7: Explain the importance of China for Timothy Brook's portrayal of global integration.

3. For students with student numbers ending in 8, 9, and 0: How do luxury articles consumed in Europe help explain "the dawn of the global world?"

Weaver (700 words) Due in the tutorial of the **tenth week.**

1. Students with student numbers ending in 1, 2, and 3: Summarize the diversity of encounters between first peoples and colonizers. Cite examples.

2. Students with student numbers ending in 4, 5, and 6: Were individuals as at least as important as governments in the history of imperial expansion? Cite examples to support your case.

3. Students with student numbers ending in 7, 8, 9, and 0: Identify and describe the types of conflicts (who clashed with whom?) on the world's settlement frontiers? Cite examples.

COURSEWARE ASSIGNMENTS:

MANDATORY QUESTIONS AND WHEN TO SUBMIT

(In all cases cite page references in footnotes or endnotes. Use full citation information in the first citation and the author and page number only thereafter. See FAQ # 11.)

1. (250 words) For all students: In the clash between the Inca empire and the Spanish warrior-adventurers, what enabled the latter to conquer with few losses? Consider "proximate" and "ultimate" causes. This must be submitted at the beginning of your tutorial in the **sixth week**.

2. (250 words) For all students: Certain Chinese dynasties pursued territorial expansion and established empires. In the eighteenth century, the Qing Empire sent armies westward into Central Asia and, along with the Russian Empire, crushed the independent remnants of the nomadic Mongols. According to Peter Perdue, how has nationalism biased the way this episode of imperialism been written about? Explain your answer. This must be submitted at the beginning of your tutorial in the **eighth week**.

LIBRARY VIDEO AND TEST

From 15 to 21 September, there will be an on-line library knowledge test. It is worth 5% of the final mark. To take the test, go on-line and access Avenue to Learn and look for 1CC3. This will be the only occasion that we use Avenue. Some material meshes with the tutorial that week.

DETAILED AGENDA: LECTURE TOPICS AND TUTORIALS

First class. 5 September: Vital tips for success at university. Course objectives: understanding the contemporary world through history.

2. Week of 9-12 September. "Eurocentric Perspectives and Organizing Concepts." These lectures will cover three major questions that resurface throughout this course: 1) What accounts for the appearance that European countries as paramount imperial powers between roughly 1500 and 1900? 2) What is an empire; what is a colony? 3) What are the fundamental challenges that empires in most ages and regions have confronted and how did rulers attempt to solve them?

3. Week of 16-19 September. "Control and Plunder: The Foundations of European Empires." Lectures this week introduce Eurasia as a heartland of empires, propose the importance of" continental axes," and illustrate these concepts with references to the Roman Empire, Byzantine Empire, and Vikings. The **tutorial** this week will offer tips on how to write history assignments. Read chapters 3, 4, and 6 of *A Pocket Guide to Writing in History*. Know the following terms and come prepared to discuss them: primary sources, secondary sources, global statements, active voice, passive voice, biased language, active reading, and plagiarism.

4. Week of 23-26 September. "The Largest Empire: Eurasian Encounters." The topics this week include the Mongol Empire, the Black Death, Europe's frontiers and reviving cities. In your tutorial for this week, submit your assignment on Alfred Crosby, *Ecological Imperialism*. In the **tutorial**, you will be led in a discussion of Crosby that considers his over-arching argument and his use of Iceland, the Holy Lands, the Canary Islands, and winds and currents to help explain colonization by European empires.

"5. Week of 30 September to 3 October. "Imperial Mixers: The Luxury Trade, Disease, the Word, and the Sword." This week the lectures will focus on the clash of empires in and around the Mediterranean. They will look at trade, alliance, and betrayal with respect to Venice and Genoa; the Islamic World and Ottoman Empire; the formation of the Hapsburg Empire. **No tutorial.**

6. Week of 7-10 October. "The Re-conquest [*Reconquisata*]: Footloose Warriors Seize Empires." This week we return to an opening question. Why Europe? We consider early modern warfare, the Portuguese Empire, the Spanish Empire in the Americas and in "the Spanish Lake" -- the Pacific Ocean. In this week's **tutorial**, the tutors will remark in general on your writing based on the first two assignments and at the start of class you will submit the short assignment on the chapters extracted from Jared Diamond's *Guns, Germs, and Steel;* there will be a brief discussion of these chapters.

7. Week of 14-17 October. "The Industrious Revolution, the Dutch, and the Company Empire." The lectures will consider the rise of Amsterdam, the reach and force of the Dutch East India Company, the rise of capitalism, and London's adoption of Dutch practices. In your **tutorial** for this week, submit your assignment on Timothy Brook, *Vermeer's Hat*. Discussion of this book will occupy the tutorial this week.

8. Week of 21-24 October. "The Landed Empire: China and the Needham Question." Joseph Needham (1900-1992) was an English scientist who wrote *Science and Civilization in China*: a multi-volume history. Some of it was based on *The Complete Collection of Illustrations and Writings of Ancient and Modern Times*, a work of nearly 6000 volumes in modern edition. It was commissioned by an early Qing emperor in 1700 and intended to be the sum of all Chinese knowledge. Needham's work leaves us with the question, why didn't China establish an overseas empire? At the start of class please submit the short assignment on sections of book chapters by Peter Perdue. Perdue explains that the Qing (1644-1912) did have an empire that was much like those established by several European powers, but it was land based. For the **tutorial** come prepared to discuss Perdue's ideas the steps that historians can take to minimize bias of the type that he criticizes.

9. 28 October (mid-term recess 30 October to 3 November; any missed material in the lectures will spill over into next week). "The Intrusive Empire: Implanting Metropolitan Values." Our consideration of Asia continues with an examination of the British Empire by looking at the East India Company, the emergent modern state, bureaucracy, the birth of the discipline of Economics, and India as a Crown colony. The **tutorial** this week involves no written assignment. Come prepared to discuss a Eurocentric bias in history and whether this can be dealt with in a reasonable way; these are topics mentioned by John Darwin in chapter 1 ("Orientations") in *After Tamerlane* (courseware). Darwin's chapter is important for understanding the place of Europe in world history.

10. Week of 4-7 November. "The Closing Acts of European Empires." During the next three weeks we will cover the final episodes of European imperial expansion. This week we look at France and Germany

in the Pacific Ocean, and the European powers' "Rush for Africa." The tutorial will review your writing based on the Brook assignment and will consider in general if lessons from previous comments have been learned. In your **tutorial** for this week, submit your assignment on Weaver. Discussion of Weaver.

11. Week of 11-14 November. "Eastward Empire." In this lecture, we consider the formation of Tsarist Russia and its expansion into the Steppes, Central Asia, and Siberia. **No tutorial.**

12. Week of 18-21 November. "The Never-ending Upheaval of Empires." These lectures consider settler colonies, property rights, and first peoples. The areas covered include the Louisiana Territory, Rupert's Land, Australia, Southern Africa, and New Zealand. The tutorial discussion will focus on chapter five ("British Kenya: The Short Life of the New Imperialism") in Timothy Parson's *The Rule of Empires*. There is no written assignment for this **tutorial**, but be prepared to discuss what he meant by the new imperialism. What is his point of view? Is the new imperialism new? How? Why did it have a short life?

13. Week of 25-28 November. "The Successor Empire?" In this last lecture on late nineteenth century empires, we look at United States abroad in the late nineteenth and early twentieth centuries. The **tutorial** will review course themes. The last assignment will be returned.

14. 2 December. Review in class.

ADDITIONAL IMPORTANT INFORMATION

FAQs

1. What are the terms and conditions of the McMaster Student Absence Form?

The MSAF is a self-reporting tool for students to report absences due to minor medical situations. The MSAF lasts up to 5 days and provides an opportunity **to request** accommodation for missed academic work; **it cannot be used retroactively** to cover missed work. If you miss a deadline without prior permission, you will receive **zero on that assignment.** With respect to the MSAF, it is up to the instructor's discretion (John Weaver) to grant an extension and to set the terms of an extension. You may be asked to write on a different topic but from the same reading. You can only submit one request per term. It is your responsibility to follow up with your instructor (John Weaver) immediately (normally within two days) regarding the extension that will be negotiated. Otherwise in this course, the MSAF is void.

2. Is there a textbook for this course?

No. The course's themes and content are conveyed best in lectures, assigned books, and courseware. This course is custom designed. However, you may find Ringrose, *Expansion and Global Interaction* useful. This book is optional. It is concise and covers many events mentioned in lectures.

3. Does this course use Avenue to Learn?

No. This course accents **formal writing** exercises and **reading books.** Time and effort are best spent focusing on reading, note taking, and polishing prose. Well-reasoned and well-documented writings are assigned in this course, and well-reasoned and well-documented submissions are expected.

4. Will the Power Point slides be available for review?

Yes. It will be possible to access the slides early in the term by accessing the History Department web page. The contents and order of the slides may change slightly as the term develops. There will also be podcasts of the lectures. These will be released from time to time.

5. Is there a participation mark for the tutorials?

No. In this course, good writing is the vital measure of performance; attendance at tutorials is necessary, however, because assignments must be submitted in the tutorials by the student and the final exam will have questions that pertain to the readings as they have been discussed in the tutorials.

6. Can assignments be submitted electronically?

No. See 5.

7. Is there a penalty for overdue assignments?

Yes. They must be submitted in the tutorial in which the subject will be discussed; late assignments will not be marked and the grade for the assignment will be zero. The exception is the one-time MSAF. See FAQ #1.

8. Are there opportunities to ask for a clarification of the course material?

Yes. Questions on the content of the lectures during the lectures are welcomed.

9. Can students write on a question or topic different from the ones assigned by student number?

No. The questions and the method of distributing them have been prepared to achieve a variety of insights in each tutorial section and to encourage students to read thoroughly the assigned books, chapters, and articles. The **questions assigned must be answered** and general statements resembling a thin book review will not suffice and could lead to an extremely low mark for that assignment.

10. Is there a mid-term?

No. A final exam will cover themes and factual information presented in the lectures and readings from throughout this course.

11. What is a Letter of Academic Accommodation?

A few students have particular perceptual conditions that adversely affect reading or writing, but ability and the will to learn remain strong. When diagnosed, certain conditions may lead to special assistance or consideration. Proposed arrangements are first suggested by Student Accessibility Services but they **must promptly be negotiated with the instructor.** I consider them during my office hours or by appointment only; **I do not sign these requests in the class room.** If you feel you would qualify for an assessment and letter, please contact Student Accessibility Services in Room B107 Student Centre.

12. Is there a preferred method for citing sources in the assignments?

Yes. You may use either endnotes or footnotes; but please note that in History we do not use the Social Sciences practices of citation.

When you cite a book for the first time in a set of footnotes or endnotes, you must provide complete information: author's name, full title of the book, publication information, and pages [eg. Alfred M. Crosby, *Ecological Imperialism: The Biological Expansion of Europe, 900-1900* (Cambridge: Cambridge University Press, 1986), 295-8.]. In subsequent citations, you may use a shortened form [eg. Crosby, *Ecological Imperialism*, 305.]

For articles, cite the author, the title of the article, the title of the journal, the volume number, the date, and the pages [Paul A. Kramer, "Power and Connection: Imperial Histories of the United States in the World," *The American Historical Review*, vol.116, number 5 (December 2011), 1361-3]. In subsequent citations, you may use a shortened form. [eg. Kramer, "Power and Connection," 1375.

Exam Date

If for a medical reason or another compelling personal reason, you miss a final examination, you must petition for a deferred exam. The authority to grant a deferral rests with the Faculty of Humanities office and is not automatic. Please consult the undergraduate calendar for details. **Holiday plans are insufficient reason to ask for a deferred exam.**

Extensions and Accommodations

Extensions or other accommodations will be determined by the instructor (TA) and will only be considered if supported by appropriate documentation. Absences of less than 5 days may be reported using the McMaster Student Absence Form (MSAF) at www.mcmaster.ca/msaf/. If you are unable to use the MSAF, you should document the absence with your faculty office. In all cases, it is YOUR responsibility to follow up with the instructor immediately to see if an extension or other accommodation will be granted, and what form it will take. There are NO automatic extensions or accommodations. In this course, please note that there are penalties for overdue work without a prior formal extension or accommodation.

Academic Dishonesty

Academic dishonesty consists of misrepresentation by deception or by other fraudulent means and can result in serious consequences, e.g. the grade of zero on an assignment, loss of credit with a notation on the transcript (notation reads: "Grade of F assigned for academic dishonesty"), and/or suspension or expulsion from the university. Sadly, every year first year history students have been found to have submitted work that was not their own. Usually, they were in a rush and thought they cut a corner just this once. Don't join them.

It is your responsibility to understand what constitutes academic dishonesty. For information on the various kinds of academic dishonesty please refer to the Academic Integrity Policy, specifically Appendix 3, located at:

http://www.mcmaster.ca/univsec/policy/AcademicIntegrity.pdf

History 1CC3

TABLE OF CONTENTS
& ACKNOWLEDGEMENTS

PAGE

Guide to Reading Jared Diamond's Chapters "Collision at Cajamarca" and "hemisphere's Colliding" from *Guns, Germs, and Steel*

1. Locate Cajamarca on a web site and note its current state of development. Are there strong continuities between past and present at Cajamarca?

2. Pizarro was seeking plunder but he was also a representative of which European monarch? Which Empire? Why is that significant for this course?

3. Diamond quotes primary sources. What are they? How do they reveal biases and the values of their writers?

4. Omissions or silences are also important to note when reading primary sources. After you have read the two chapters, think about likely omissions. What are some observations that the writers might have left out of their accounts? Explain.

5. In future courses in many fields you are likely to encounter the term "agency." Often it means the capacity of oppressed peoples to sustain some realms of influence or control in their lives; it can also mean that we should not simply see conquered peoples solely as victims but note that they had their own wars and vassals. How is agency represented in these chapters?

6. What does Diamond suggest are some limitations to the concept of agency?

7. Central to Diamond's organization of world history is his division of causes into proximate and ultimate. What precisely is his argument? List examples.

CHAPTER 3

COLLISION AT CAJAMARCA

T HE BIGGEST POPULATION SHIFT OF MODERN TIMES HAS been the colonization of the New World by Europeans, and the resulting conquest, numerical reduction, or complete disappearance of most groups of Native Americans (American Indians). As I explained in Chapter 1, the New World was initially colonized around or before 11,000 B.C. by way of Alaska, the Bering Strait, and Siberia. Complex agricultural societies gradually arose in the Americas far to the south of that entry route, developing in complete isolation from the emerging complex societies of the Old World. After that initial colonization from Asia, the sole well-attested further contacts between the New World and Asia involved only hunter-gatherers living on opposite sides of the Bering Strait, plus an inferred transpacific voyage that introduced the sweet potato from South America to Polynesia.

As for contacts of New World peoples with Europe, the sole early ones involved the Norse who occupied Greenland in very small numbers between A.D. 986 and about 1500. But those Norse visits had no discernible impact on Native American societies. Instead, for practical purposes the collision of advanced Old World and New World societies began abruptly in A.D. 1492, with Christopher Columbus's "discovery" of Caribbean islands densely populated by Native Americans.

The most dramatic moment in subsequent European–Native American relations was the first encounter between the Inca emperor Atahuallpa and the Spanish conquistador Francisco Pizarro at the Peruvian highland town of Cajamarca on November 16, 1532. Atahuallpa was absolute monarch of the largest and most advanced state in the New World, while Pizarro represented the Holy Roman Emperor Charles V (also known as King Charles I of Spain), monarch of the most powerful state in Europe. Pizarro, leading a ragtag group of 168 Spanish soldiers, was in unfamiliar terrain, ignorant of the local inhabitants, completely out of touch with the nearest Spaniards (1,000 miles to the north in Panama) and far beyond the reach of timely reinforcements. Atahuallpa was in the middle of his own empire of millions of subjects and immediately surrounded by his army of 80,000 soldiers, recently victorious in a war with other Indians. Nevertheless, Pizarro captured Atahuallpa within a few minutes after the two leaders first set eyes on each other. Pizarro proceeded to hold his prisoner for eight months, while extracting history's largest ransom in return for a promise to free him. After the ransom—enough gold to fill a room 22 feet long by 17 feet wide to a height of over 8 feet—was delivered, Pizarro reneged on his promise and executed Atahuallpa.

Atahuallpa's capture was decisive for the European conquest of the Inca Empire. Although the Spaniards' superior weapons would have assured an ultimate Spanish victory in any case, the capture made the conquest quicker and infinitely easier. Atahuallpa was revered by the Incas as a sun-god and exercised absolute authority over his subjects, who obeyed even the orders he issued from captivity. The months until his death gave Pizarro time to dispatch exploring parties unmolested to other parts of the Inca Empire, and to send for reinforcements from Panama. When fighting between Spaniards and Incas finally did commence after Atahuallpa's execution, the Spanish forces were more formidable.

Thus, Atahuallpa's capture interests us specifically as marking the decisive moment in the greatest collision of modern history. But it is also of more general interest, because the factors that resulted in Pizarro's seizing Atahuallpa were essentially the same ones that determined the outcome of many similar collisions between colonizers and native peoples elsewhere in the modern world. Hence Atahuallpa's capture offers us a broad window onto world history.

WHAT UNFOLDED THAT day at Cajamarca is well known, because it was recorded in writing by many of the Spanish participants. To get a

flavor of those events, let us relive them by weaving together excerpts from eyewitness accounts by six of Pizarro's companions, including his brothers Hernando and Pedro:

"The prudence, fortitude, military discipline, labors, perilous navigations, and battles of the Spaniards—vassals of the most invincible Emperor of the Roman Catholic Empire, our natural King and Lord—will cause joy to the faithful and terror to the infidels. For this reason, and for the glory of God our Lord and for the service of the Catholic Imperial Majesty, it has seemed good to me to write this narrative, and to send it to Your Majesty, that all may have a knowledge of what is here related. It will be to the glory of God, because they have conquered and brought to our holy Catholic Faith so vast a number of heathens, aided by His holy guidance. It will be to the honor of our Emperor because, by reason of his great power and good fortune, such events happened in his time. It will give joy to the faithful that such battles have been won, such provinces discovered and conquered, such riches brought home for the King and for themselves; and that such terror has been spread among the infidels, such admiration excited in all mankind.

"For when, either in ancient or modern times, have such great exploits been achieved by so few against so many, over so many climes, across so many seas, over such distances by land, to subdue the unseen and unknown? Whose deeds can be compared with those of Spain? Our Spaniards, being few in number, never having more than 200 or 300 men together, and sometimes only 100 and even fewer, have, in our times, conquered more territory than has ever been known before, or than all the faithful and infidel princess possess. I will only write, at present, of what befell in the conquest, and I will not write much, in order to avoid prolixity.

"Governor Pizarro wished to obtain intelligence from some Indians who had come from Cajamarca, so he had them tortured. They confessed that they had heard that Atahuallpa was waiting for the Governor at Cajamarca. The Governor then ordered us to advance. On reaching the entrance to Cajamarca, we saw the camp of Atahuallpa at a distance of a league, in the skirts of the mountains. The Indians' camp looked like a very beautiful city. They had so many tents that we were all filled with great apprehension. Until then, we had never seen anything like this in the Indies. It filled all our Spaniards with fear and confusion. But we could not show any fear or turn back, for if the Indians had sensed any weakness in us, even the Indians that we were bringing with us as guides would have killed us. So we made a show of good spirits, and after carefully observing the town and the tents, we descended into the valley and entered Cajamarca.

"We talked a lot among ourselves about what to do. All of us were full of fear, because we were so few in number and we had penetrated so far into a land where we could not hope to receive reinforcements. We all met with the Governor to debate what we should undertake the next day. Few of us slept that night, and we kept watch in the square of Cajamarca, looking at the campfires of the Indian army. It was a frightening sight. Most of the campfires were on a hillside and so close to each other that it looked like the sky brightly studded with stars. There was no distinction that night between the mighty and the lowly, or between foot soldiers and horsemen. Everyone carried out sentry duty fully armed. So too did the good old Governor, who went about encouraging his men. The Governor's brother Hernando Pizarro estimated the number of Indian soldiers there at 40,000, but he was telling a lie just to encourage us, for there were actually more than 80,000 Indians.

"On the next morning a messenger from Atahuallpa arrived, and the Governor said to him, 'Tell your lord to come when and how he pleases, and that, in what way soever he may come I will receive him as a friend and brother. I pray that he may come quickly, for I desire to see him. No harm or insult will befall him.'

"The Governor concealed his troops around the square at Cajamarca, dividing the cavalry into two portions of which he gave the command of one to his brother Hernando Pizarro and the command of the other to Hernando de Soto. In like manner he divided the infantry, he himself taking one part and giving the other to his brother Juan Pizarro. At the same time, he ordered Pedro de Candia with two or three infantrymen to go with trumpets to a small fort in the plaza and to station themselves there with a small piece of artillery. When all the Indians, and Atahuallpa with them, had entered the Plaza, the Governor would give a signal to Candia and his men, after which they should start firing the gun, and the trumpets should sound, and at the sound of the trumpets the cavalry should dash out of the large court where they were waiting hidden in readiness.

"At noon Atahuallpa began to draw up his men and to approach. Soon we saw the entire plain full of Indians, halting periodically to wait for more Indians who kept filing out of the camp behind them. They kept filing out in separate detachments into the afternoon. The front detach-

ments were now close to our camp, and still more troops kept issuing from the camp of the Indians. In front of Atahuallpa went 2,000 Indians who swept the road ahead of him, and these were followed by the warriors, half of whom were marching in the fields on one side of him and half on the other side.

"First came a squadron of Indians dressed in clothes of different colors, like a chessboard. They advanced, removing the straws from the ground and sweeping the road. Next came three squadrons in different dresses, dancing and singing. Then came a number of men with armor, large metal plates, and crowns of gold and silver. So great was the amount of furniture of gold and silver which they bore, that it was a marvel to observe how the sun glinted upon it. Among them came the figure of Atahuallpa in a very fine litter with the ends of its timbers covered in silver. Eighty lords carried him on their shoulders, all wearing a very rich blue livery. Atahuallpa himself was very richly dressed, with his crown on his head and a collar of large emeralds around his neck. He sat on a small stool with a rich saddle cushion resting on his litter: The litter was lined with parrot feathers of many colors and decorated with plates of gold and silver.

"Behind Atahuallpa came two other litters and two hammocks, in which were some high chiefs, then several squadrons of Indians with crowns of gold and silver. These Indian squadrons began to enter the plaza to the accompaniment of great songs, and thus entering they occupied every part of the plaza. In the meantime all of us Spaniards were waiting ready, hidden in a courtyard, full of fear. Many of us urinated without noticing it, out of sheer terror. On reaching the center of the plaza, Atahuallpa remained in his litter on high, while his troops continued to file in behind him.

"Governor Pizarro now sent Friar Vicente de Valverde to go speak to Atahuallpa, and to require Atahuallpa in the name of God and of the King of Spain that Atahuallpa subject himself to the law of our Lord Jesus Christ and to the service of His Majesty the King of Spain. Advancing with a cross in one hand and the Bible in the other hand, and going among the Indian troops up to the place where Atahuallpa was, the Friar thus addressed him: 'I am a Priest of God, and I teach Christians the things of God, and in like manner I come to teach you. What I teach is that which God says to us in this Book. Therefore, on the part of God and of the Christians, I beseech you to be their friend, for such is God's will, and it will be for your good.'

"Atahuallpa asked for the Book, that he might look at it, and the Friar gave it to him closed. Atahuallpa did not know how to open the Book, and the Friar was extending his arm to do so, when Atahuallpa, in great anger, gave him a blow on the arm, not wishing that it should be opened. Then he opened it himself, and, without any astonishment at the letters and paper he threw it away from him five or six paces, his face a deep crimson.

"The Friar returned to Pizarro, shouting, 'Come out! Come out, Christians! Come at these enemy dogs who reject the things of God. That tyrant has thrown my book of holy law to the ground! Did you not see what happened? Why remain polite and servile toward this over-proud dog when the plains are full of Indians? March out against him, for I absolve you!'

"The governor then gave the signal to Candia, who began to fire off the guns. At the same time the trumpets were sounded, and the armored Spanish troops, both cavalry and infantry, sallied forth out of their hiding places straight into the mass of unarmed Indians crowding the square, giving the Spanish battle cry, 'Santiago!' We had placed rattles on the horses to terrify the Indians. The booming of the guns, the blowing of the trumpets, and the rattles on the horses threw the Indians into panicked confusion. The Spaniards fell upon them and began to cut them to pieces. The Indians were so filled with fear that they climbed on top of one another, formed mounds, and suffocated each other. Since they were unarmed, they were attacked without danger to any Christian. The cavalry rode them down, killing and wounding, and following in pursuit. The infantry made so good an assault on those that remained that in a short time most of them were put to the sword.

"The Governor himself took his sword and dagger, entered the thick of the Indians with the Spaniards who were with him, and with great bravery reached Atahuallpa's litter. He fearlessly grabbed Atahuallpa's left arm and shouted 'Santiago!,' but he could not pull Atahuallpa out of his litter because it was held up high. Although we killed the Indians who held the litter, others at once took their places and held it aloft, and in this manner we spent a long time in overcoming and killing Indians. Finally seven or eight Spaniards on horseback spurred on their horses, rushed upon the litter from one side, and with great effort they heaved it over on its side. In that way Atahuallpa was captured, and the Governor took Atahuallpa

to his lodging. The Indians carrying the litter, and those escorting Atahuallpa, never abandoned him: all died around him.

"The panic-stricken Indians remaining in the square, terrified at the firing of the guns and at the horses—something they had never seen—tried to flee from the square by knocking down a stretch of wall and running out onto the plain outside. Our cavalry jumped the broken wall and charged into the plain, shouting, 'Chase those with the fancy clothes! Don't let any escape! Spear them!' All of the other Indian soldiers whom Atahuallpa had brought were a mile from Cajamarca ready for battle, but not one made a move, and during all this not one Indian raised a weapon against a Spaniard. When the squadrons of Indians who had remained in the plain outside the town saw the other Indians fleeing and shouting, most of them too panicked and fled. It was an astonishing sight, for the whole valley for 15 or 20 miles was completely filled with Indians. Night had already fallen, and our cavalry were continuing to spear Indians in the fields, when we heard a trumpet calling for us to reassemble at camp.

"If night had not come on, few out of the more than 40,000 Indian troops would have been left alive. Six or seven thousand Indians lay dead, and many more had their arms cut off and other wounds. Atahuallpa himself admitted that we had killed 7,000 of his men in that battle. The man killed in one of the litters was his minister, the lord of Chincha, of whom he was very fond. All those Indians who bore Atahuallpa's litter appeared to be high chiefs and councillors. They were all killed, as well as those Indians who were carried in the other litters and hammocks. The lord of Cajamarca was also killed, and others, but their numbers were so great that they could not be counted, for all who came in attendance on Atahuallpa were great lords. It was extraordinary to see so powerful a ruler captured in so short a time, when he had come with such a mighty army. Truly, it was not accomplished by our own forces, for there were so few of us. It was by the grace of God, which is great.

"Atahuallpa's robes had been torn off when the Spaniards pulled him out of his litter. The Governor ordered clothes to be brought to him, and when Atahuallpa was dressed, the Governor ordered Atahuallpa to sit near him and soothed his rage and agitation at finding himself so quickly fallen from his high estate. The Governor said to Atahuallpa, 'Do not take it as an insult that you have been defeated and taken prisoner, for with the Christians who come with me, though so few in number, I have conquered greater kingdoms than yours, and have defeated other more powerful lords than you, imposing upon them the dominion of the Emperor, whose vassal I am, and who is King of Spain and of the universal world. We come to conquer this land by his command, that all may come to a knowledge of God and of His Holy Catholic Faith; and by reason of our good mission, God, the Creator of heaven and earth and of all things in them, permits this, in order that you may know Him and come out from the bestial and diabolical life that you lead. It is for this reason that we, being so few in number, subjugate that vast host. When you have seen the errors in which you live, you will understand the good that we have done you by coming to your land by order of his Majesty the King of Spain. Our Lord permitted that your pride should be brought low and that no Indian should be able to offend a Christian.' "

LET US NOW trace the chain of causation in this extraordinary confrontation, beginning with the immediate events. When Pizarro and Atahuallpa met at Cajamarca, why did Pizarro capture Atahuallpa and kill so many of his followers, instead of Atahuallpa's vastly more numerous forces capturing and killing Pizarro? After all, Pizarro had only 62 soldiers mounted on horses, along with 106 foot soldiers, while Atahuallpa commanded an army of about 80,000. As for the antecedents of those events, how did Atahuallpa come to be at Cajamarca at all? How did Pizarro come to be there to capture him, instead of Atahuallpa's coming to Spain to capture King Charles I? Why did Atahuallpa walk into what seems to us, with the gift of hindsight, to have been such a transparent trap? Did the factors acting in the encounter of Atahuallpa and Pizarro also play a broader role in encounters between Old World and New World peoples and between other peoples?

Why did Pizarro capture Atahuallpa? Pizarro's military advantages lay in the Spaniards' steel swords and other weapons, steel armor, guns, and horses. To those weapons, Atahuallpa's troops, without animals on which to ride into battle, could oppose only stone, bronze, or wooden clubs, maces, and hand axes, plus slingshots and quilted armor. Such imbalances of equipment were decisive in innumerable other confrontations of Europeans with Native Americans and other peoples.

The sole Native Americans able to resist European conquest for many

centuries were those tribes that reduced the military disparity by acquiring and mastering both horses and guns. To the average white American, the word "Indian" conjures up an image of a mounted Plains Indian brandishing a rifle, like the Sioux warriors who annihilated General George Custer's U.S. Army battalion at the famous battle of the Little Big Horn in 1876. We easily forget that horses and rifles were originally unknown to Native Americans. They were brought by Europeans and proceeded to transform the societies of Indian tribes that acquired them. Thanks to their mastery of horses and rifles, the Plains Indians of North America, the Araucanian Indians of southern Chile, and the Pampas Indians of Argentina fought off invading whites longer than did any other Native Americans, succumbing only to massive army operations by white governments in the 1870s and 1880s.

Today, it is hard for us to grasp the enormous numerical odds against which the Spaniards' military equipment prevailed. At the battle of Cajamarca recounted above, 168 Spaniards crushed a Native American army 500 times more numerous, killing thousands of natives while not losing a single Spaniard. Time and again, accounts of Pizarro's subsequent battles with the Incas, Cortés's conquest of the Aztecs, and other early European campaigns against Native Americans describe encounters in which a few dozen European horsemen routed thousands of Indians with great slaughter. During Pizarro's march from Cajamarca to the Inca capital of Cuzco after Atahuallpa's death, there were four such battles: at Jauja, Vilcashuaman, Vilcaconga, and Cuzco. Those four battles involved a mere 80, 30, 110, and 40 Spanish horsemen, respectively, in each case ranged against thousands or tens of thousands of Indians.

These Spanish victories cannot be written off as due merely to the help of Native American allies, to the psychological novelty of Spanish weapons and horses, or (as is often claimed) to the Incas' mistaking Spaniards for their returning god Viracocha. The initial successes of both Pizarro and Cortés did attract native allies. However, many of them would not have become allies if they had not already been persuaded, by earlier devastating successes of unassisted Spaniards, that resistance was futile and that they should side with the likely winners. The novelty of horses, steel weapons, and guns undoubtedly paralyzed the Incas at Cajamarca, but the battles after Cajamarca were fought against determined resistance by Inca armies that had already seen Spanish weapons and horses. Within half a dozen years of the initial conquest, Incas mounted two desperate, large-scale, well-prepared rebellions against the Spaniards. All those efforts failed because of the Spaniards' far superior armament.

By the 1700s, guns had replaced swords as the main weapon favoring European invaders over Native Americans and other native peoples. For example, in 1808 a British sailor named Charlie Savage equipped with muskets and excellent aim arrived in the Fiji Islands. The aptly named Savage proceeded single-handedly to upset Fiji's balance of power. Among his many exploits, he paddled his canoe up a river to the Fijian village of Kasavu, halted less than a pistol shot's length from the village fence, and fired away at the undefended inhabitants. His victims were so numerous that surviving villagers piled up the bodies to take shelter behind them, and the stream beside the village was red with blood. Such examples of the power of guns against native peoples lacking guns could be multiplied indefinitely.

In the Spanish conquest of the Incas, guns played only a minor role. The guns of those times (so-called harquebuses) were difficult to load and fire, and Pizarro had only a dozen of them. They did produce a big psychological effect on those occasions when they managed to fire. Far more important were the Spaniards' steel swords, lances, and daggers, strong sharp weapons that slaughtered thinly armored Indians. In contrast, Indian blunt clubs, while capable of battering and wounding Spaniards and their horses, rarely succeeded in killing them. The Spaniards' steel or chain mail armor and, above all, their steel helmets usually provided an effective defense against club blows, while the Indians' quilted armor offered no protection against steel weapons.

The tremendous advantage that the Spaniards gained from their horses leaps out of the eyewitness accounts. Horsemen could easily outride Indian sentries before the sentries had time to warn Indian troops behind them, and could ride down and kill Indians on foot. The shock of a horse's charge, its maneuverability, the speed of attack that it permitted, and the raised and protected fighting platform that it provided left foot soldiers nearly helpless in the open. Nor was the effect of horses due only to the terror that they inspired in soldiers fighting against them for the first time. By the time of the great Inca rebellion of 1536, the Incas had learned how best to defend themselves against cavalry, by ambushing and annihilating Spanish horsemen in narrow passes. But the Incas, like all other foot soldiers, were never able to defeat cavalry in the open. When Quizo Yupan-

qui, the best general of the Inca emperor Manco, who succeeded Atahuallpa, besieged the Spaniards in Lima in 1536 and tried to storm the city, two squadrons of Spanish cavalry charged a much larger Indian force on flat ground, killed Quizo and all of his commanders in the first charge, and routed his army. A similar cavalry charge of 26 horsemen routed the best troops of Emperor Manco himself, as he was besieging the Spaniards in Cuzco.

The transformation of warfare by horses began with their domestication around 4000 B.C., in the steppes north of the Black Sea. Horses permitted people possessing them to cover far greater distances than was possible on foot, to attack by surprise, and to flee before a superior defending force could be gathered. Their role at Cajamarca thus exemplifies a military weapon that remained potent for 6,000 years, until the early 20th century, and that was eventually applied on all the continents. Not until the First World War did the military dominance of cavalry finally end. When we consider the advantages that Spaniards derived from horses, steel weapons, and armor against foot soldiers without metal, it should no longer surprise us that Spaniards consistently won battles against enormous odds.

How did Atahuallpa come to be at Cajamarca? Atahuallpa and his army came to be at Cajamarca because they had just won decisive battles in a civil war that left the Incas divided and vulnerable. Pizarro quickly appreciated those divisions and exploited them. The reason for the civil war was that an epidemic of smallpox, spreading overland among South American Indians after its arrival with Spanish settlers in Panama and Colombia, had killed the Inca emperor Huayna Capac and most of his court around 1526, and then immediately killed his designated heir, Ninan Cuyuchi. Those deaths precipitated a contest for the throne between Atahuallpa and his half brother Huascar. If it had not been for the epidemic, the Spaniards would have faced a united empire.

Atahuallpa's presence at Cajamarca thus highlights one of the key factors in world history: diseases transmitted to peoples lacking immunity by invading peoples with considerable immunity. Smallpox, measles, influenza, typhus, bubonic plague, and other infectious diseases endemic in Europe played a decisive role in European conquests, by decimating many peoples on other continents. For example, a smallpox epidemic devastated the Aztecs after the failure of the first Spanish attack in 1520 and killed Cuitláhuac, the Aztec emperor who briefly succeeded Montezuma.

Throughout the Americas, diseases introduced with Europeans spread from tribe to tribe far in advance of the Europeans themselves, killing an estimated 95 percent of the pre-Columbian Native American population. The most populous and highly organized native societies of North America, the Mississippian chiefdoms, disappeared in that way between 1492 and the late 1600s, even before Europeans themselves made their first settlement on the Mississippi River. A smallpox epidemic in 1713 was the biggest single step in the destruction of South Africa's native San people by European settlers. Soon after the British settlement of Sydney in 1788, the first of the epidemics that decimated Aboriginal Australians began. A well-documented example from Pacific islands is the epidemic that swept over Fiji in 1806, brought by a few European sailors who struggled ashore from the wreck of the ship Argo. Similar epidemics marked the histories of Tonga, Hawaii, and other Pacific islands.

I do not mean to imply, however, that the role of disease in history was confined to paving the way for European expansion. Malaria, yellow fever, and other diseases of tropical Africa, India, Southeast Asia, and New Guinea furnished the most important obstacle to European colonization of those tropical areas.

How did Pizarro come to be at Cajamarca? Why didn't Atahuallpa instead try to conquer Spain? Pizarro came to Cajamarca by means of European maritime technology, which built the ships that took him across the Atlantic from Spain to Panama, and then in the Pacific from Panama to Peru. Lacking such technology, Atahuallpa did not expand overseas out of South America.

In addition to the ships themselves, Pizarro's presence depended on the centralized political organization that enabled Spain to finance, build, staff, and equip the ships. The Inca Empire also had a centralized political organization, but that actually worked to its disadvantage, because Pizarro seized the Inca chain of command intact by capturing Atahuallpa. Since the Inca bureaucracy was so strongly identified with its godlike absolute monarch, it disintegrated after Atahuallpa's death. Maritime technology coupled with political organization was similarly essential for European expansions to other continents, as well as for expansions of many other peoples.

A related factor bringing Spaniards to Peru was the existence of writing. Spain possessed it, while the Inca Empire did not. Information could be spread far more widely, more accurately, and in more detail by writing

than it could be transmitted by mouth. That information, coming back to Spain from Columbus's voyages and from Cortés's conquest of Mexico, sent Spaniards pouring into the New World. Letters and pamphlets supplied both the motivation and the necessary detailed sailing directions. The first published report of Pizarro's exploits, by his companion Captain Cristóbal de Mena, was printed in Seville in April 1534, a mere nine months after Atahuallpa's execution. It became a best-seller, was rapidly translated into other European languages, and sent a further stream of Spanish colonists to tighten Pizarro's grip on Peru.

Why did Atahuallpa walk into the trap? In hindsight, we find it astonishing that Atahuallpa marched into Pizarro's obvious trap at Cajamarca. The Spaniards who captured him were equally surprised at their success. The consequences of literacy are prominent in the ultimate explanation.

The immediate explanation is that Atahuallpa had very little information about the Spaniards, their military power, and their intent. He derived that scant information by word of mouth, mainly from an envoy who had visited Pizarro's force for two days while it was en route inland from the coast. That envoy saw the Spaniards at their most disorganized, told Atahuallpa that they were not fighting men, and that he could tie them all up if given 200 Indians. Understandably, it never occurred to Atahuallpa that the Spaniards were formidable and would attack him without provocation.

In the New World the ability to write was confined to small elites among some peoples of modern Mexico and neighboring areas far to the north of the Inca Empire. Although the Spanish conquest of Panama, a mere 600 miles from the Incas' northern boundary, began already in 1510, no knowledge even of the Spaniards' existence appears to have reached the Incas until Pizarro's first landing on the Peruvian coast in 1527. Atahuallpa remained entirely ignorant about Spain's conquests of Central America's most powerful and populous Indian societies.

As surprising to us today as Atahuallpa's behavior leading to his capture is his behavior thereafter. He offered his famous ransom in the naive belief that, once paid off, the Spaniards would release him and depart. He had no way of understanding that Pizarro's men formed the spearhead of a force bent on permanent conquest, rather than an isolated raid.

Atahuallpa was not alone in these fatal miscalculations. Even after Atahuallpa had been captured, Francisco Pizarro's brother Hernando Pizarro deceived Atahuallpa's leading general, Chalcuchima, commanding a large army, into delivering himself to the Spaniards. Chalcuchima's miscalculation marked a turning point in the collapse of Inca resistance, a moment almost as significant as the capture of Atahuallpa himself. The Aztec emperor Montezuma miscalculated even more grossly when he took Cortés for a returning god and admitted him and his tiny army into the Aztec capital of Tenochtitlán. The result was that Cortés captured Montezuma, then went on to conquer Tenochtitlán and the Aztec Empire.

On a mundane level, the miscalculations by Atahuallpa, Chalcuchima, Montezuma, and countless other Native American leaders deceived by Europeans were due to the fact that no living inhabitants of the New World had been to the Old World, so of course they could have had no specific information about the Spaniards. Even so, we find it hard to avoid the conclusion that Atahuallpa "should" have been more suspicious, if only his society had experienced a broader range of human behavior. Pizarro too arrived at Cajamarca with no information about the Incas other than what he had learned by interrogating the Inca subjects he encountered in 1527 and 1531. However, while Pizarro himself happened to be illiterate, he belonged to a literate tradition. From books, the Spaniards knew of many contemporary civilizations remote from Europe, and about several thousand years of European history. Pizarro explicitly modeled his ambush of Atahuallpa on the successful strategy of Cortés.

In short, literacy made the Spaniards heirs to a huge body of knowledge about human behavior and history. By contrast, not only did Atahuallpa have no conception of the Spaniards themselves, and no personal experience of any other invaders from overseas, but he also had not even heard (or read) of similar threats to anyone else, anywhere else, anytime previously in history. That gulf of experience encouraged Pizarro to set his trap and Atahuallpa to walk into it.

THUS, PIZARRO'S CAPTURE OF Atahuallpa illustrates the set of proximate factors that resulted in Europeans' colonizing the New World instead of Native Americans' colonizing Europe. Immediate reasons for Pizarro's success included military technology based on guns, steel weapons, and horses; infectious diseases endemic in Eurasia; European maritime technology; the centralized political organization of European states; and writing. The title of this book will serve as shorthand for those proximate factors, which also enabled modern Europeans to conquer peoples of other conti-

nents. Long before anyone began manufacturing guns and steel, others of those same factors had led to the expansions of some non-European peoples, as we shall see in later chapters.

But we are still left with the fundamental question why all those immediate advantages came to lie more with Europe than with the New World. Why weren't the Incas the ones to invent guns and steel swords, to be mounted on animals as fearsome as horses, to bear diseases to which European lacked resistance, to develop oceangoing ships and advanced political organization, and to be able to draw on the experience of thousands of years of written history? Those are no longer the questions of proximate causation that this chapter has been discussing, but questions of ultimate causation that will take up the next two parts of this book.

CHAPTER 18

HEMISPHERES COLLIDING

THE LARGEST POPULATION REPLACEMENT OF THE LAST 13,000 years has been the one resulting from the recent collision between Old World and New World societies. Its most dramatic and decisive moment, as we saw in Chapter 3, occurred when Pizarro's tiny army of Spaniards captured the Inca emperor Atahuallpa, absolute ruler of the largest, richest, most populous, and most advanced Native American state. Atahuallpa's capture symbolizes the European conquest of the Americas, because the same mix of proximate factors that caused it was also responsible for European conquests of other Native American societies. Let us now return to that collision of hemispheres, applying what we have learned since Chapter 3. The basic question to be answered is: why did Europeans reach and conquer the lands of Native Americans, instead of vice versa? Our starting point will be a comparison of Eurasian and Native American societies as of A.D. 1492, the year of Columbus's "discovery" of the Americas.

OUR COMPARISON BEGINS with food production, a major determinant of local population size and societal complexity—hence an ultimate factor behind the conquest. The most glaring difference between American and Eurasian food production involved big domestic mammal species. In Chapter 9 we encountered Eurasia's 13 species, which became its chief source of animal protein (meat and milk), wool, and hides, its main mode of land transport of people and goods, its indispensable vehicles of warfare, and (by drawing plows and providing manure) a big enhancer of crop production. Until waterwheels and windmills began to replace Eurasia's mammals in medieval times, they were also the major source of its "industrial" power beyond human muscle power—for example, for turning grindstones and operating water lifts. In contrast, the Americas had only one species of big domestic mammal, the llama / alpaca, confined to a small area of the Andes and the adjacent Peruvian coast. While it was used for meat, wool, hides, and goods transport, it never yielded milk for human consumption, never bore a rider, never pulled a cart or a plow, and never served as a power source or vehicle of warfare.

That's an enormous set of differences between Eurasian and Native American societies—due largely to the Late Pleistocene extinction (extermination?) of most of North and South America's former big wild mammal species. If it had not been for those extinctions, modern history might have taken a different course. When Cortés and his bedraggled adventurers landed on the Mexican coast in 1519, they might have been driven into the sea by thousands of Aztec cavalry mounted on domesticated native American horses. Instead of the Aztecs' dying of smallpox, the Spaniards might have been wiped out by American germs transmitted by disease-resistant Aztecs. American civilizations resting on animal power might have been sending their own conquistadores to ravage Europe. But those hypothetical outcomes were foreclosed by mammal extinctions thousands of years earlier.

Those extinctions left Eurasia with many more wild candidates for domestication than the Americas offered. Most candidates disqualify themselves as potential domesticates for any of half a dozen reasons. Hence Eurasia ended up with its 13 species of big domestic mammals and the Americas with just its one very local species. Both hemispheres also had domesticated species of birds and small mammals—the turkey, guinea pig, and Muscovy duck very locally and the dog more widely in the Americas; chickens, geese, ducks, cats, dogs, rabbits, honeybees, silkworms, and some others in Eurasia. But the significance of all those species of small domestic animals was trivial compared with that of the big ones. Eurasia and the Americas also differed with respect to plant food pro-

[handwritten margin note: lack of animal power]

duction, though the disparity here was less marked than for animal food production. In 1492 agriculture was widespread in Eurasia. Among the few Eurasian hunter-gatherers lacking both crops and domestic animals were the Ainu of northern Japan, Siberian societies without reindeer, and small hunter-gatherer groups scattered through the forests of India and tropical Southeast Asia and trading with neighboring farmers. Some other Eurasian societies, notably the Central Asian pastoralists and the reindeer-herding Lapps and Samoyeds of the Arctic, had domestic animals but little or no agriculture. Virtually all other Eurasian societies engaged in agriculture as well as in herding animals.

Agriculture was also widespread in the Americas, but hunter-gatherers occupied a larger fraction of the Americas' area than of Eurasia's. Those regions of the Americas without food production included all of northern North America and southern South America, the Canadian Great Plains, and all of western North America except for small areas of the U.S. Southwest that supported irrigation agriculture. It is striking that the areas of Native America without food production included what today, after Europeans' arrival, are some of the most productive farmlands and pastures of both North and South America: the Pacific states of the United States, Canada's wheat belt, the pampas of Argentina, and the Mediterranean zone of Chile. The former absence of food production in these lands was due entirely to their local paucity of domesticable wild animals and plants, and to geographic and ecological barriers that prevented the crops and the few domestic animal species of other parts of the Americas from arriving. Those lands became productive not only for European settlers but also, in some cases, for Native Americans, as soon as Europeans introduced suitable domestic animals and crops. For instance, Native American societies became renowned for their mastery of horses, and in some cases of cattle and sheepherding, in parts of the Great Plains, the western United States, and the Argentine pampas. Those mounted plains warriors and Navajo sheepherders and weavers now figure prominently in white Americans' image of American Indians, but the basis for that image was created only after 1492. These examples demonstrate that the sole missing ingredients required to sustain food production in large areas of the Americas were domestic animals and crops themselves.

In those parts of the Americas that did support Native American agriculture, it was constrained by five major disadvantages vis-à-vis Eurasian agriculture: widespread dependence on protein-poor corn, instead of

Eurasia's diverse and protein-rich cereals; hand planting of individual seeds, instead of broadcast sowing; tilling by hand instead of plowing by animals, which enables one person to cultivate a much larger area, and which also permits cultivation of some fertile but tough soils and sods that are difficult to till by hand (such as those of the North American Great Plains); lack of animal manuring to increase soil fertility; and just human muscle power, instead of animal power, for agricultural tasks such as threshing, grinding, and irrigation. These differences suggest that Eurasian agriculture as of 1492 may have yielded on the average more calories and protein per person-hour of labor than Native American agriculture did.

SUCH DIFFERENCES IN food production constituted a major ultimate cause of the disparities between Eurasian and Native American societies. Among the resulting proximate factors behind the conquest, the most important included differences in germs, technology, political organization, and writing. Of these, the one linked most directly to the differences in food production was germs. The infectious diseases that regularly visited crowded Eurasian societies, and to which many Eurasians consequently developed immune or genetic resistance, included all of history's most lethal killers: smallpox, measles, influenza, plague, tuberculosis, typhus, cholera, malaria, and others. Against that grim list, the sole crowd infectious diseases that can be attributed with certainty to pre-Columbian Native American societies were nonsyphilitic treponemas. (As I explained in Chapter 11, it remains uncertain whether syphilis arose in Eurasia or in the Americas, and the claim that human tuberculosis was present in the Americas before Columbus is in my opinion unproven.)

This continental difference in harmful germs resulted paradoxically from the difference in useful livestock. Most of the microbes responsible for the infectious diseases of crowded human societies evolved from very similar ancestral microbes causing infectious diseases of the domestic animals with which food producers began coming into daily close contact around 10,000 years ago. Eurasia harbored many domestic animal species and hence developed many such microbes, while the Americas had very few of each. Other reasons why Native American societies evolved so few lethal microbes were that villages, which provide ideal breeding grounds for epidemic diseases, arose thousands of years later in the Americas than in Eurasia; and that the three regions of the New World supporting urban societies (the Andes, Mesoamerica, and the U.S. Southeast) were never connected by fast, high-volume trade on the scale that brought plague, influenza, and possibly smallpox to Europe from Asia. As a result, even malaria and yellow fever, the infectious diseases that eventually became major obstacles to European colonization of the American tropics, and that posed the biggest barrier to the construction of the Panama Canal, are not American diseases at all but are caused by microbes of Old World tropical origin, introduced to the Americas by Europeans.

Rivaling germs as proximate factors behind Europe's conquest of the Americas were the differences in all aspects of technology. These differences stemmed ultimately from Eurasia's much longer history of densely populated, economically specialized, politically centralized, interacting and competing societies dependent on food production. Five areas of technology may be singled out:

First, metals—initially copper, then bronze, and finally iron—were used for tools in all complex Eurasian societies as of 1492. In contrast, although copper, silver, gold, and alloys were used for ornaments in the Andes and some other parts of the Americas, stone and wood and bone were still the principal materials for tools in all Native American societies, which made only limited local use of copper tools.

Second, military technology was far more potent in Eurasia than in the Americas. European weapons were steel swords, lances, and daggers, supplemented by small firearms and artillery, while body armor and helmets were also made of solid steel or else of chain mail. In place of steel, Native Americans used clubs and axes of stone or wood (occasionally copper in the Andes), slings, bows and arrows, and quilted armor, constituting much less effective protection and weaponry. In addition, Native American armies had no animals to oppose to horses, whose value for assaults and fast transport gave Europeans an overwhelming advantage until some Native American societies themselves adopted them.

Third, Eurasian societies enjoyed a huge advantage in their sources of power to operate machines. The earliest advance over human muscle power was the use of animals—cattle, horses, and donkeys—to pull plows and to turn wheels for grinding grain, raising water, and irrigating or draining fields. Waterwheels appeared in Roman times and then proliferated, along with tidal mills and windmills, in the Middle Ages. Coupled to systems of geared wheels, those engines harnessing water and wind power were used not only to grind grain and move water but also to serve myriad

manufacturing purposes, including crushing sugar, driving blast furnace bellows, grinding ores, making paper, polishing stone, pressing oil, producing salt, producing textiles, and sawing wood. It is conventional to define the Industrial Revolution arbitrarily as beginning with the harnessing of steam power in 18th-century England, but in fact an industrial revolution based on water and wind power had begun already in medieval times in many parts of Europe. As of 1492, all of those operations to which animal, water, and wind power were being applied in Eurasia were still being carried out by human muscle power in the Americas.

Long before the wheel began to be used in power conversion in Eurasia, it had become the basis of most Eurasian land transport—not only for animal-drawn vehicles but also for human-powered wheelbarrows, which enabled one or more people, still using just human muscle power, to transport much greater weights than they could have otherwise. Wheels were also adopted in Eurasian pottery making and in clocks. None of those uses of the wheel was adopted in the Americas, where wheels are attested only in Mexican ceramic toys.

The remaining area of technology to be mentioned is sea transport. Many Eurasian societies developed large sailing ships, some of them capable of sailing against the wind and crossing the ocean, equipped with sextants, magnetic compasses, sternpost rudders, and cannons. In capacity, speed, maneuverability, and seaworthiness, those Eurasian ships were far superior to the rafts that carried out trade between the New World's most advanced societies, those of the Andes and Mesoamerica. Those rafts sailed with the wind along the Pacific coast. Pizarro's ship easily ran down and captured such a raft on his first voyage toward Peru.

IN ADDITION TO their germs and technology, Eurasian and Native American societies differed in their political organization. By late medieval or Renaissance times, most of Eurasia had come under the rule of organized states. Among these, the Habsburg, Ottoman, and Chinese states, the Mogul state of India, and the Mongol state at its peak in the 13th century started out as large polyglot amalgamations formed by the conquest of other states. For that reason they are generally referred to as empires. Many Eurasian states and empires had official religions that contributed to state cohesion, being invoked to legitimize the political leadership and to sanction wars against other peoples. Tribal and band societies

Table 18.1 summarizes approximate dates of the appearance of key developments in the main "homelands" of each hemisphere (the Fertile Crescent and China in Eurasia, the Andes and Amazonia and Mesoamerica in the Americas). It also includes the trajectory for the minor New World homeland of the eastern United States, and that for England, which is not a homeland at all but is listed to illustrate how rapidly developments spread from the Fertile Crescent.

This table is sure to horrify any knowledgeable scholar, because it reduces exceedingly complex histories to a few seemingly precise dates. In reality, all of those dates are merely attempts to label arbitrary points along a continuum. For example, more significant than the date of the first metal tool found by some archaeologist is the time when a significant fraction of all tools was made of metal, but how common must metal tools be to rate as "widespread"? Dates for the appearance of the same development may differ among different parts of the same homeland. For instance, within the Andean region pottery appears about 1,300 years earlier in coastal Ecuador (3100 B.C.) than in Peru (1800 B.C.). Some dates, such as those for the rise of chiefdoms, are more difficult to infer from the archaeological record than are dates of artifacts like pottery or metal tools. Some of the dates in Table 18.1 are very uncertain, especially those for the onset of American food production. Nevertheless, as long as one understands that the table is a simplification, it is useful for comparing continental histories.

The table suggests that food production began to provide a large fraction of human diets around 5,000 years earlier in the Eurasian homelands than in those of the Americas. A caveat must be mentioned immediately: while there is no doubt about the antiquity of food production in Eurasia, there is controversy about its onset in the Americas. In particular, archaeologists often cite considerably older claimed dates for domesticated plants at Coxcatlán Cave in Mexico, at Guitarrero Cave in Peru, and at some other American sites than the dates given in the table. Those claims are now being reevaluated for several reasons: recent direct radiocarbon dating of crop remains themselves has in some cases been yielding younger dates; the older dates previously reported were based instead on charcoal thought to be contemporaneous with the plant remains, but possibly not so; and the status of some of the older plant remains as crops or just as collected wild plants is uncertain. Still, even if plant domestication did begin earlier in the Americas than the dates shown in Table 18.1, agricul-

in Eurasia were largely confined to the Arctic reindeer herders, the Siberian hunter-gatherers, and the hunter-gatherer enclaves in the Indian subcontinent and tropical Southeast Asia.

The Americas had two empires, those of the Aztecs and Incas, which resembled their Eurasian counterparts in size, population, polyglot make-up, official religions, and origins in the conquest of smaller states. In the Americas those were the sole two political units capable of mobilizing resources for public works or war on the scale of many Eurasian states, whereas seven European states (Spain, Portugal, England, France, Holland, Sweden, and Denmark) had the resources to acquire American colonies between 1492 and 1666. The Americas also held many chiefdoms (some of them virtually small states) in tropical South America, Mesoamerica beyond Aztec rule, and the U.S. Southeast. The rest of the Americas was organized only at the tribal or band level.

The last proximate factor to be discussed is writing. Most Eurasian states had literate bureaucracies, and in some a significant fraction of the populace other than bureaucrats was also literate. Writing empowered European societies by facilitating political administration and economic exchanges, motivating and guiding exploration and conquest, and making available a range of information and human experience extending into remote places and times. In contrast, use of writing in the Americas was confined to the elite in a small area of Mesoamerica. The Inca Empire employed an accounting system and mnemonic device based on knots (termed quipu), but it could not have approached writing as a vehicle for transmitting detailed information.

THUS, EURASIAN SOCIETIES in the time of Columbus enjoyed big advantages over Native American societies in food production, germs, technology (including weapons), political organization, and writing. These were the main factors tipping the outcome of the post-Columbian collisions. But those differences as of A.D. 1492 represent just one snapshot of historical trajectories that had extended over at least 13,000 years in the Americas, and over a much longer time in Eurasia. For the Americas, in particular, the 1492 snapshot captures the end of the independent trajectory of Native Americans. Let us now trace out the earlier stages of those trajectories.

TABLE 18.1 Historical Trajectories of Eurasia and the Americas

Approximate Date of Adoption	Eurasia			Native America			
	Fertile Crescent	China	England	Andes	Amazonia	Mesoamerica	Eastern U.S.
Plant domestication	8500 B.C.	by 7500 B.C.	3500 B.C.	by 3000 B.C.	3000 B.C.	by 3000 B.C.	2500 B.C.
Animal domestication	8000 B.C.	by 7500 B.C.	3500 B.C.	3500 B.C.	?	500 B.C.	—
Pottery	7000 B.C.	by 7500 B.C.	3500 B.C.	3100–1800 B.C.	6000 B.C.	1500 B.C.	2500 B.C.
Villages	9000 B.C.	by 7500 B.C.	3000 B.C.	3100–1800 B.C.	6000 B.C.	1500 B.C.	500 B.C.
Chiefdoms	5500 B.C.	4000 B.C.	2500 B.C.	by 1500 B.C.	A.D. 1	1500 B.C.	200 B.C.
Widespread metal tools or artifacts (copper and/or bronze)	4000 B.C.	2000 B.C.	2000 B.C.	A.D. 1000	—	—	—
States	3700 B.C.	2000 B.C.	500 A.D.	A.D. 1	—	300 B.C.	—
Writing	3200 B.C.	by 1300 B.C.	A.D. 43	—	—	600 B.C.	—
Widespread iron tools	900 B.C.	500 B.C.	650 B.C.	—	—	—	—

This table gives approximate dates of widespread adoption of significant developments in three Eurasian and four Native American areas. Dates for animal domestication neglect dogs, which were domesticated earlier than food-producing animals in both Eurasia and the Americas. Chiefdoms are inferred from archaeological evidence, such as ranked burials, architecture, and settlement patterns. The table greatly simplifies a complex mass of historical facts: see the text for some of the many important caveats.

ture surely did not provide the basis for most human calorie intake and sedentary existence in American homelands until much later than in Eurasian homelands.

As we saw in Chapters 5 and 10, only a few relatively small areas of each hemisphere acted as a "homeland" where food production first arose and from which it then spread. Those homelands were the Fertile Crescent and China in Eurasia, and the Andes and Amazonia, Mesoamerica, and the eastern United States in the Americas. The rate of spread of key developments is especially well understood for Europe, thanks to the many archaeologists at work there. As Table 18.1 summarizes for England, once food production and village living had arrived from the Fertile Crescent after a long lag (5,000 years), the subsequent lag for England's adoption of chiefdoms, states, writing, and especially metal tools was much shorter: 2,000 years for the first widespread metal tools of copper and bronze, and only 250 years for widespread iron tools. Evidently, it was much easier for one society of already sedentary farmers to "borrow" metallurgy from another such society than for nomadic hunter-gatherers to "borrow" food production from sedentary farmers (or to be replaced by the farmers).

WHY WERE THE trajectories of all key developments shifted to later dates in the Americas than in Eurasia? Four groups of reasons suggest themselves: the later start, more limited suite of wild animals and plants available for domestication, greater barriers to diffusion, and possibly smaller or more isolated areas of dense human populations in the Americas than in Eurasia.

As for Eurasia's head start, humans have occupied Eurasia for about a million years, far longer than they have lived in the Americas. According to the archaeological evidence discussed in Chapter 1, humans entered the Americas at Alaska only around 12,000 B.C., spread south of the Canadian ice sheets as Clovis hunters a few centuries before 11,000 B.C., and reached the southern tip of South America by 10,000 B.C. Even if the dis-

been evolving to utilize wild cereals were available to the first cereal farmers of the Fertile Crescent. In contrast, the first settlers of the Americas arrived in Alaska with equipment appropriate to the Siberian Arctic tundra. They had to invent for themselves the equipment suitable to each new habitat they encountered. That technology lag may have contributed significantly to the delay in Native American developments.

An even more obvious factor behind the delay was the wild animals and plants available for domestication. As I discussed in Chapter 6, when hunter-gatherers adopt food production, it is not because they foresee the potential benefits awaiting their remote descendants but because incipient food production begins to offer advantages over the hunter-gatherer lifestyle. Early food production was less competitive with hunting-gathering in the Americas than in the Fertile Crescent or China, partly owing to the Americas' virtual lack of domesticable wild mammals. Hence early American farmers remained dependent on wild animals for animal protein and necessarily remained part-time hunter-gatherers, whereas in both the Fertile Crescent and China animal domestication followed plant domestication very closely in time to create a food producing package that quickly won out over hunting-gathering. In addition, Eurasian domestic animals made Eurasian agriculture itself more competitive by providing fertilizer, and eventually by drawing plows.

Features of American wild plants also contributed to the lesser competitiveness of Native American food production. That conclusion is clearest for the eastern United States, where less than a dozen crops were domesticated, including small-seeded grains but no large-seeded grains, pulses, fiber crops, or cultivated fruit or nut trees. It is also clear for Mesoamerica's staple grain of corn, which spread to become a dominant crop elsewhere in the Americas as well. Whereas the Fertile Crescent's wild wheat and barley evolved into crops with minimal changes and within a few centuries, wild teosinte may have required several thousand years to evolve into corn, having to undergo drastic changes in its reproductive biology and energy allocation to seed production, loss of the seed's rock-hard casings, and an enormous increase in cob size.

As a result, even if one accepts the recently postulated later dates for the onset of Native American plant domestication, about 1,500 or 2,000 years would have elapsed between that onset (about 3000–2500 B.C.) and widespread year-round villages (1800–500 B.C.) in Mesoamerica, the inland Andes, and the eastern United States. Native American farming

puted claims of older human occupation sites in the Americas prove valid, those postulated pre-Clovis inhabitants remained for unknown reasons very sparsely distributed and did not launch a Pleistocene proliferation of hunter-gatherer societies with expanding populations, technology, and art as in the Old World. Food production was already arising in the Fertile Crescent only 1,500 years after the time when Clovis-derived hunter-gatherers were just reaching southern South America.

Several possible consequences of that Eurasian head start deserve consideration. First, could it have taken a long time after 11,000 B.C. for the Americas to fill up with people? When one works out the likely numbers involved, one finds that this effect would make only a trivial contribution to the Americas' 5,000-year lag in food-producing villages. The calculations given in Chapter 1 tell us that even if a mere 100 pioneering Native Americans had crossed the Canadian border into the lower United States and increased at a rate of only 1 percent per year, they would have saturated the Americas with hunter-gatherers within 1,000 years. Spreading south at a mere one mile per month, those pioneers would have reached the southern tip of South America only 700 years after crossing the Canadian border. Those postulated rates of spread and of population increase are very low compared with actual known rates for peoples occupying previously uninhabited or sparsely inhabited lands. Hence the Americas were probably fully occupied by hunter-gatherers within a few centuries of the arrival of the first colonists.

Second, could a large part of the 5,000-year lag have represented the time that the first Americans required to become familiar with the new local plant species, animal species, and rock sources that they encountered? If we can again reason by analogy with New Guinean and Polynesian hunter-gatherers and farmers occupying previously unfamiliar environments—such as Maori colonists of New Zealand or Tudawhe colonists of New Guinea's Karimui Basin—the colonists probably discovered the best rock sources and learned to distinguish useful from poisonous wild plants and animals in much less than a century.

Third, what about Eurasians' head start in developing locally appropriate technology? The early farmers of the Fertile Crescent and China were heirs to the technology that behaviorially modern *Homo sapiens* had been developing to exploit local resources in those areas for tens of thousands of years. For instance, the stone sickles, underground storage pits, and other technology that hunter-gatherers of the Fertile Crescent had

served for a long time just as a small supplement to food acquisition by hunting-gathering, and supported only a sparse population. If one accepts the traditional, earlier dates for the onset of American plant domestication, then 5,000 years instead of 1,500 or 2,000 years elapsed before food production supported villages. In contrast, villages were closely associated in time with the rise of food production in much of Eurasia. (The hunter-gatherer lifestyle itself was sufficiently productive to support villages even before the adoption of agriculture in parts of both hemispheres, such as Japan and the Fertile Crescent in the Old World, and coastal Ecuador and Amazonia in the New World.) The limitations imposed by locally available domesticates in the New World are well illustrated by the transformations of Native American societies themselves when other crops or animals arrived, whether from elsewhere in the Americas or from Eurasia. Examples include the effects of corn's arrival in the eastern United States and Amazonia, the llama's adoption in the northern Andes after its domestication to the south, and the horse's appearance in many parts of North and South America.

In addition to Eurasia's head start and wild animal and plant species, developments in Eurasia were also accelerated by the easier diffusion of animals, plants, ideas, technology, and people in Eurasia than in the Americas, as a result of several sets of geographic and ecological factors. Eurasia's east-west major axis, unlike the Americas' north-south major axis, permitted diffusion without change in latitude and associated environmental variables. In contrast to Eurasia's consistent east-west breadth, the New World was constricted over the whole length of Central America and especially at Panama. Not least, the Americas were more fragmented by areas unsuitable for food production or for dense human populations. These ecological barriers included the rain forests of the Panamanian isthmus separating Mesoamerican societies from Andean and Amazonian societies; the deserts of northern Mexico separating Mesoamerica from U.S. southwestern and southeastern societies; dry areas of Texas separating the U.S. Southwest from the Southeast; and the deserts and high mountains fencing off U.S. Pacific coast areas that would otherwise have been suitable for food production. As a result, there was no diffusion of domestic animals, writing, or political entities, and limited or slow diffusion of crops and technology, between the New World centers of Mesoamerica, the eastern United States, and the Andes and Amazonia.

Some specific consequences of these barriers within the Americas

deserve mention. Food production never diffused from the U.S. Southwest and Mississippi Valley to the modern American breadbaskets of California and Oregon, where Native American societies remained hunter-gatherers merely because they lacked appropriate domesticates. The llama, guinea pig, and potato of the Andean highlands never reached the Mexican highlands, so Mesoamerica and North America remained without domestic mammals except for dogs. Conversely, the domestic sunflower of the eastern United States never reached Mesoamerica, and the domestic turkey of Mesoamerica never made it to South America or the eastern United States. Mesoamerican corn and beans took 3,000 and 4,000 years, respectively, to cover the 700 miles from Mexico's farmlands to the eastern U.S. farmlands. After corn's arrival in the eastern United States, seven centuries more passed before the development of a corn variety productive in North American climates triggered the Mississippian emergence. Corn, beans, and squash may have taken several thousand years to spread from Mesoamerica to the U.S. Southwest. While Fertile Crescent crops spread west and east sufficiently fast to preempt independent domestication of the same species or else domestication of closely related species elsewhere, the barriers within the Americas gave rise to many such parallel domestications of crops.

As striking as these effects of barriers on crop and livestock diffusion are the effects on other features of human societies. Alphabets of ultimately eastern Mediterranean origin spread throughout all complex societies of Eurasia, from England to Indonesia, except for areas of East Asia where derivatives of the Chinese writing system took hold. In contrast, the New World's sole writing systems, those of Mesoamerica, never spread to the complex Andean and eastern U.S. societies that might have adopted them. The wheels invented in Mesoamerica as parts of toys never met the llamas domesticated in the Andes, to generate wheeled transport for the New World. From east to west in the Old World, the Macedonian Empire and the Roman Empire both spanned 3,000 miles, the Mongol Empire 6,000 miles. But the empires and states of Mesoamerica had no political relations with, and apparently never even heard of, the chiefdoms of the eastern United States 700 miles to the north or the empires and states of the Andes 1,200 miles to the south.

The greater geographic fragmentation of the Americas compared with Eurasia is also reflected in distributions of languages. Linguists agree in grouping all but a few Eurasian languages into about a dozen language

TABLE 18.2 Language Expansions in the Old World

Inferred Date	Language Family or Language	Expansion	Ultimate Driving Force
6000 or 4000 B.C.	Indo-European	Ukraine or Anatolia→Europe, C. Asia, India	food production or horse-based pastoralism
6000 B.C.–2000 B.C.	Elamo-Dravidian	Iran→India	food production
4000 B.C.–present	Sino-Tibetan	Tibetan Plateau, N. China→ S. China, tropical S.E. Asia	food production
3000 B.C.–1000 B.C.	Austronesian	S. China→Indonesia, Pacific islands	food production
3000 B.C.–A.D. 1000	Bantu	Nigeria and Cameroon →S. Africa	food production
3000 B.C.–A.D. 1	Austroasiatic	S. China→tropical S.E. Asia, India	food production
1000 B.C.–A.D. 1500	Tai-Kadai, Miao-Yao	S. China→tropical S.E. Asia	food production
A.D. 892	Hungarian	Ural Mts.→ Hungary	horse-based pastoralism
A.D. 1000–A.D. 1300	Altaic (Mongol, Turkish)	Asian steppes→ Europe, Turkey, China, India	horse-based pastoralism
A.D. 1480–A.D. 1638	Russian	European Russia →Asiatic Siberia	food production

families, each consisting of up to several hundred related languages. For example, the Indo-European language family, which includes English as well as French, Russian, Greek, and Hindi, comprises about 144 languages. Quite a few of those families occupy large contiguous areas—in the case of Indo-European, the area encompassing most of Europe east through much of western Asia to India. Linguistic, historical, and archaeological evidence combines to make clear that each of these large, contiguous distributions stems from a historical expansion of an ancestral language, followed by subsequent local linguistic differentiation to form a family of related languages (Table 18.2). Most such expansions appear to be attributable to the advantages that speakers of the ancestral language, belonging to food-producing societies, held over hunter-gatherers. We already discussed such historical expansions in Chapters 16 and 17 for the Sino-Tibetan, Austronesian, and other East Asian language families.

Among major expansions of the last millennium are those that carried Indo-European languages from Europe to the Americas and Australia, the Russian language from eastern Europe across Siberia, and Turkish (a language of the Altaic family) from Central Asia westward to Turkey.

With the exception of the Eskimo-Aleut language family of the American Arctic and the Na-Dene language family of Alaska, northwestern Canada, and the U.S. Southwest, the Americas lack examples of large-scale language expansions widely accepted by linguists. Most linguists specializing in Native American languages do not discern large, clear-cut groupings other than Eskimo-Aleut and Na-Dene. At most, they consider the evidence sufficient only to group other Native American languages (variously estimated to number from 600 to 2,000) into a hundred or more language groups or isolated languages. A controversial minority view is that of the linguist Joseph Greenberg, who groups all Native American languages other than Eskimo-Aleut and Na-Dene languages into a single large family, termed Amerind, with about a dozen subfamilies.

Some of Greenberg's subfamilies, and some groupings recognized by more-traditional linguists, may turn out to be legacies of New World population expansions driven in part by food production. These legacies may include the Uto-Aztecan languages of Mesoamerica and the western United States, the Oto-Manguean languages of Mesoamerica, the Natchez-Muskogean languages of the U.S. Southeast, and the Arawak languages of the West Indies. But the difficulties that linguists have in agreeing

18

on groupings of Native American languages reflect the difficulties that complex Native American societies themselves faced in expanding within the New World. Had any food-producing Native American peoples succeeded in spreading far with their crops and livestock and rapidly replacing hunter-gatherers over a large area, they would have left legacies of easily recognized language families, as in Eurasia, and the relationships of Native American languages would not be so controversial.

Thus, we have identified three sets of ultimate factors that tipped the advantage to European invaders of the Americas: Eurasia's long head start on human settlement; its more effective food production, resulting from greater availability of domesticable wild plants and especially of animals; and its less formidable geographic and ecological barriers to intracontinental diffusion. A fourth, more speculative ultimate factor is suggested by some puzzling non-inventions in the Americas: the non-inventions of writing and wheels in complex Andean societies, despite a time depth of those societies approximately equal to that of complex Mesoamerican societies that did make those inventions; and wheels' confinement to toys and their eventual disappearance in Mesoamerica, where they could presumably have been useful in human-powered wheelbarrows, as in China. These puzzles remind one of equally puzzling non-inventions, or else disappearances of inventions, in small isolated societies, including Aboriginal Tasmania, Aboriginal Australia, Japan, Polynesian islands, and the American Arctic. Of course, the Americas in aggregate are anything but small: their combined area is fully 76 percent that of Eurasia, and their human population as of A.D. 1492 was probably also a large fraction of Eurasia's. But the Americas, as we have seen, are broken up into "islands" of societies with tenuous connections to each other. Perhaps the histories of Native American wheels and writing exemplify the principles illustrated in a more extreme form by true island societies.

AFTER AT LEAST 13,000 years of separate developments, advanced American and Eurasian societies finally collided within the last thousand years. Until then, the sole contacts between human societies of the Old and the New Worlds had involved the hunter-gatherers on opposite sides of the Bering Strait.

There were no Native American attempts to colonize Eurasia, except at the Bering Strait, where a small population of Inuit (Eskimos) derived from

Alaska established itself across the strait on the opposite Siberian coast. The first documented Eurasian attempt to colonize the Americas was by the Norse at Arctic and sub-Arctic latitudes (Figure 18.1). Norse from Norway colonized Iceland in A.D. 874, then Norse from Iceland colonized Greenland in A.D. 986, and finally Norse from Greenland repeatedly visited the northeastern coast of North America between about A.D. 1000 and 1350. The sole Norse archaeological site discovered in the Americas is on Newfoundland, possibly the region described as Vinland in Norse sagas, but these also mention landings evidently farther north, on the coasts of Labrador and Baffin Island.

Iceland's climate permitted herding and extremely limited agriculture, and its area was sufficient to support a Norse-derived population that has persisted to this day. But most of Greenland is covered by an ice cap, and even the two most favorable coastal fjords were marginal for Norse food production. The Greenland Norse population never exceeded a few thousand. It remained dependent on imports of food and iron from Norway, and of timber from the Labrador coast. Unlike Easter Island and other

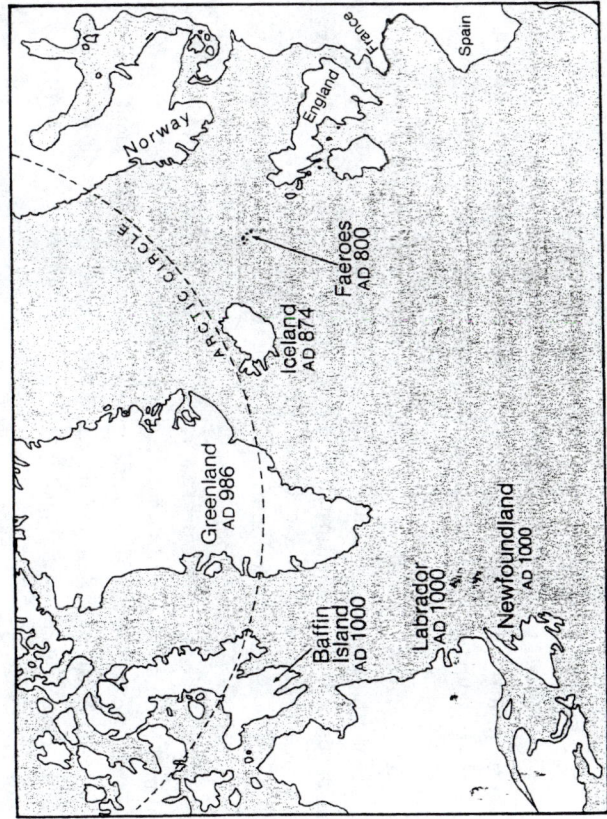

Figure 18.1. The Norse expansion from Norway across the North Atlantic, with dates or approximate dates when each area was reached.

and Indian hunter-gatherers, the world's greatest masters of Arctic survival skills.

THE SECOND EURASIAN attempt to colonize the Americas succeeded because it involved a source, target, latitude, and time that allowed Europe's potential advantages to be exerted effectively. Spain, unlike Norway, was rich and populous enough to support exploration and subsidize colonies. Spanish landfalls in the Americas were at subtropical latitudes highly suitable for food production, based at first mostly on Native American crops but also on Eurasian domestic animals, especially cattle and horses. Spain's transatlantic colonial enterprise began in 1492, at the end of a century of rapid development of European oceangoing ship technology, which by then incorporated advances in navigation, sails, and ship design developed by Old World societies (Islam, India, China, and Indonesia) in the Indian Ocean. As a result, ships built and manned in Spain itself were able to sail to the West Indies; there was nothing equivalent to the Greenland bottleneck that had throttled Norse colonization. Spain's New World colonies were soon joined by those of half a dozen other European states.

The first European settlements in the Americas, beginning with the one founded by Columbus in 1492, were in the West Indies. The island Indians, whose estimated population at the time of their "discovery" exceeded a million, were rapidly exterminated on most islands by disease, dispossession, enslavement, warfare, and casual murder. Around 1508 the first colony was founded on the American mainland, at the Isthmus of Panama. Conquest of the two large mainland empires, those of the Aztecs and Incas, followed in 1519–1520 and 1532–1533, respectively. In both conquests European-transmitted epidemics (probably smallpox) made major contributions, by killing the emperors themselves, as well as a large fraction of the population. The overwhelming military superiority of even tiny numbers of mounted Spaniards, together with their political skills at exploiting divisions within the native population, did the rest. European conquest of the remaining native states of Central America and northern South America followed during the 16th and 17th centuries.

As for the most advanced native societies of North America, those of the U.S. Southeast and the Mississippi River system, their destruction was

---

remote Polynesian islands, Greenland could not support a self-sufficient food-producing society, though it did support self-sufficient Inuit hunter-gatherer populations before, during, and after the Norse occupation period. The populations of Iceland and Norway themselves were too small and too poor for them to continue their support of the Greenland Norse population.

In the Little Ice Age that began in the 13th century, the cooling of the North Atlantic made food production in Greenland, and Norse voyaging to Greenland from Norway or Iceland, even more marginal than before. The Greenlanders' last known contact with Europeans came in 1410 with an Icelandic ship that arrived after being blown off course. When Europeans finally began again to visit Greenland in 1577, its Norse colony no longer existed, having evidently disappeared without any record during the 15th century.

But the coast of North America lay effectively beyond the reach of ships sailing directly from Norway itself, given Norse ship technology of the period A.D. 986–1410. The Norse visits were instead launched from the Greenland colony, separated from North America only by the 200-mile width of Davis Strait. However, the prospect of that tiny marginal colony's sustaining an exploration, conquest, and settlement of the Americas was nil. Even the sole Norse site located on Newfoundland apparently represents no more than a winter camp occupied by a few dozen people for a few years. The Norse sagas describe attacks on their Vinland camp by people termed Skraelings, evidently either Newfoundland Indians or Dorset Eskimos.

The fate of the Greenland colony, medieval Europe's most remote outpost, remains one of archaeology's romantic mysteries. Did the last Greenland Norse starve to death, attempt to sail off, intermarry with Eskimos, or succumb to disease or Eskimo arrows? While those questions of proximate cause remain unanswered, the ultimate reasons why Norse colonization of Greenland and America failed are abundantly clear. It failed because the source (Norway), the targets (Greenland and Newfoundland), and the time (A.D. 984–1410) guaranteed that Europe's potential advantages of food production, technology, and political organization could not be applied effectively. At latitudes too high for much food production, the iron tools of a few Norse, weakly supported by one of Europe's poorer states, were no match for the stone, bone, and wooden tools of Eskimo

accomplished largely by germs alone, introduced by early European explorers and advancing ahead of them. As Europeans spread throughout the Americas, many other native societies, such as the Mandans of the Great Plains and the Sadlermiut Eskimos of the Arctic, were also wiped out by disease, without need for military action. Populous native societies not thereby eliminated were destroyed in the same way the Aztecs and Incas had been—by full-scale wars, increasingly waged by professional European soldiers and their native allies. Those soldiers were backed by the political organizations initially of the European mother countries, then of the European colonial governments in the New World, and finally of the independent neo-European states that succeeded the colonial governments.

Smaller native societies were destroyed more casually, by small-scale raids and murders carried out by private citizens. For instance, California's native hunter-gatherers initially numbered about 200,000 in aggregate, but they were splintered among a hundred tribelets, none of which required a war to be defeated. Most of those tribelets were killed off or dispossessed during or soon after the California gold rush of 1848–52, when large numbers of immigrants flooded the state. As one example, the Yahi tribelet of northern California, numbering about 2,000 and lacking firearms, was destroyed in four raids by armed white settlers: a dawn raid on a Yahi village surprised by 17 settlers on August 6, 1865; a massacre of 33 Yahis tracked to a ravine in 1866; a massacre of about 30 Yahis trapped in a cave around 1867; and a final massacre of about 30 Yahis trapped in another cave by 4 cowboys around 1868. Many Amazonian Indian groups were similarly eliminated by private settlers during the rubber boom of the late 19th and early 20th centuries. The final stages of the conquest are being played out in the present decade, as the Yanomamo and other Amazonian Indian societies that remain independent are succumbing to disease, being murdered by miners, or being brought under control by missionaries or government agencies.

The end result has been the elimination of populous Native American societies from most temperate areas suitable for European food production and physiology. In North America those that survived as sizable intact communities now live mostly on reservations or other lands considered undesirable for European food production and mining, such as the Arctic and arid areas of the U.S. West. Native Americans in many tropical areas have been replaced by immigrants from the Old World tropics (especially

black Africans, along with Asian Indians and Javanese in Suriname).

In parts of Central America and the Andes, the Native Americans were originally so numerous that, even after epidemics and wars, much of the population today remains Native American or mixed. That is especially true at high altitudes in the Andes, where genetically European women have physiological difficulties even in reproducing, and where native Andean crops still offer the most suitable basis for food production. However, even where Native Americans do survive, there has been extensive replacement of their culture and languages with those of the Old World. Of the hundreds of Native American languages originally spoken in North America, all except 187 are no longer spoken at all, and 149 of these last 187 are moribund in the sense that they are being spoken only by old people and no longer learned by children. Of the approximately 40 New World nations, all now have an Indo-European language or creole as the official language. Even in the countries with the largest surviving Native American populations, such as Peru, Bolivia, Mexico, and Guatemala, a glance at photographs of political and business leaders shows that they are disproportionately Europeans, while several Caribbean nations have black African leaders and Guyana has had Asian Indian leaders.

The original Native American population has been reduced by a debated large percentage: estimates for North America range up to 95 percent. But the total human population of the Americas is now approximately ten times what it was in 1492, because of arrivals of Old World peoples (Europeans, Africans, and Asians). The Americas' population now consists of a mixture of peoples originating from all continents except Australia. That demographic shift of the last 500 years—the most massive shift on any continent except Australia—has its ultimate roots in developments between about 11,000 B.C. and A.D. 1.

Guide to Reading John Darwin's Chapter "Orientations"
from *After Tamerlane*

1. What characteristics did Tamerlane have in common with the Mongols?

2. Explain why he called his book *After Tamerlane*.

3. What countries currently comprise Central Asia?

4. Europeans reached new worlds by seas, but what geographic features contributed to the rapid formation of the extensive Arab-Islamic Caliphate, the Mongol Empire, and Tamerlane's conquests? The answer is not explicitly stated in this reading but can be deduced.

5. What concepts does Darwin use to describe our contemporary world?

6. What does Darwin think of studies that consider Empires from the perspective of how Europeans used language to depict peoples?

7. After Tamerlane, the world became 'modern,' according to Darwin. What does he think is the essential feature of our modern world? What are some of the details that make up this essence?

8. What is linear history?

9. How does Darwin retain the great significance of Europe while trying to avoid making Europe the centre of world history?

10. What is meant by 'modernity'? What does modernity mean to you?

11. Does this chapter build on primary or secondary sources? How would you describe this form of historical writing?

It had encouraged a remarkable movement of people, trade and ideas around the waist of Eurasia, along the great grassy corridor of steppe, and Mongol rule may have served as the catalyst for commercial and intellectual change in an age of general economic expansion.[3] The Mongols even permitted the visits of West European emissaries hoping to build an anti-Muslim alliance and win Christian converts. But by the early fourteenth century the effort to preserve a grand imperial confederation had all but collapsed. The internecine wars between the 'Ilkhanate' rulers in Iran, the Golden Horde and the Chagatai, and the fall of the Yuan in China (by 1368), marked the end of the Mongol experiment in Eurasian empire.

Tamerlane's conquests were partly an effort to retrieve this lost empire. But his methods were different. Much of his warfare seemed mainly designed to wreck any rivals for control of the great trunk road of Eurasian commerce, on whose profits his empire was built. Also, his power was pivoted more on command of the 'sown' than on mastery of the steppe: his armies were made up not just of mounted bowmen (the classic Mongol formula), but of infantry, artillery, heavy cavalry and even an elephant corps. His system of rule was a form of absolutism, in which the loyalty of his tribal followers was balanced against the devotion of his urban and agrarian subjects. Tamerlane claimed also to be the 'Shadow of God' (among his many titles), wreaking vengeance upon the betrayers and backsliders of the Islamic faith. Into his chosen imperial capital at Samarkand, close to his birth-place, he poured the booty of his conquests, and there he fashioned the architectural monuments that proclaimed the splendour of his reign. The 'Timurid' model was to have a lasting influence upon the idea of empire across the whole breadth of Middle Eurasia.

But, despite his ferocity, his military genius and his shrewd adapta-tion of tribal politics to his imperial purpose, Tamerlane's system fell apart at his death. As he himself may have grasped intuitively, it was no longer possible to rule the sown from the steppe and build a Eurasian empire on the old foundations of Mongol military power. The Ottomans, the Mamluk state in Egypt and Syria, the Muslim sultanate in northern India, and above all China were too resilient to be swept away by his lightning campaigns. Indeed Tamerlane's death marked in several ways the end of a long phase in global history. His

AFTER TAMERLANE

In 1401 the great Islamic historian Ibn Khaldun (1332–1406) was in the city of Damascus, then under siege by the mighty Tamerlane. Eager to meet the famous conqueror of the day, he was lowered from the walls in a basket and received in Tamerlane's camp. There he had a series of conversations with a ruler he described (in his autobio-graphy) as 'one of the greatest and mightiest of kings . . . addicted to debate and argument about what he knows and does not know'.[1] Ibn Khaldun may have seen in Tamerlane the saviour of the Arab–Muslim civilization for whose survival he feared. But four years later Tamerlane died on the road to China, whose conquest he had planned.

Tamerlane (sometimes Timur, or Timurlenk, 'Timur the Lame' – hence his European name) was a phenomenon who became a legend. He was born, probably in the 1330s, into a lesser clan of the Turkic-Mongol tribal confederation the Chagatai, one of the four great div-isions into which the Mongol empire of Genghis (Chinggis) Khan had been split up at his death, in 1227. By 1370 he had made himself master of the Chagatai. Between 1380 and 1390 he embarked upon the conquest of Iran, Mesopotamia (modern Iraq), Armenia and Georgia. In 1390 he invaded the Russian lands, returning a few years later to wreck the capital of the Golden Horde, the Mongol regime in modern South Russia. In 1398 he led a vast plundering raid into North India, crushing its Muslim rulers and demolishing Delhi. Then in 1400 he returned to the Middle East to capture Aleppo and Damas-cus (Ibn Khaldun escaped its massacre), before defeating and captur-ing the Ottoman sultan Bayazet at the Battle of Ankara in 1402. It was only after that that he turned east on his final and abortive campaign.

Despite his reputation as a bloodthirsty tyrant, and the undoubted savagery of his predatory conquests, Tamerlane was a transitional figure in Eurasian history.[2] His conquests were an echo of the great Mongol empire forged by Genghis Khan and his sons. That empire had extended from modern Iran to China, and as far north as Moscow.

empire was the last real attempt to challenge the partition of Eurasia between the states of the Far West, Islamic Middle Eurasia and Confucian East Asia. Secondly, his political experiments and ultimate failure revealed that power had begun to shift back decisively from the nomad empires to the settled states. Thirdly, the collateral damage that Tamerlane inflicted on Middle Eurasia, and the disproportionate influence that tribal societies continued to wield there, helped (if only gradually) to tilt the Old World's balance in favour of the Far East and Far West, at the expense of the centre. Lastly, his passing coincided with the first signs of a change in the existing pattern of long-distance trade, the East–West route that he had fought to control. Within a few decades of his death, the idea of a world empire ruled from Samarkand had become fantastic. The discovery of the sea as a global commons offering maritime access to every part of the world transformed the economics and geopolitics of empire. It was to take three centuries before that new world order became plainly visible. But after Tamerlane no world-conqueror arose to dominate Eurasia, and Tamerlane's Eurasia no longer encompassed almost all the known world.

GLOBAL HISTORIES

In this book we traverse a vast historical landscape in pursuit of three themes. The first is the growth of global 'connectedness' into the intensified form that we call 'globalization'. The second is the part that was played in this process by the power of Europe (and later the 'West') and through the means of empire. The third is the resilience of many of Eurasia's other states and cultures in the face of Europe's expansion. Each of these factors has played a critical part in shaping the world that became by the twentieth century a vast semi-unified system of economics and politics, a common arena from which no state, society, economy or culture was able to remain entirely aloof.

No matter how detailed the subject or obscure the topic, histories are written to help to explain how we got where we are. Of course, historians often disagree with each other's accounts, and one of the reasons is the conflict of opinion about the nature of the 'present' –

the end product of history. To add to the difficulty, we constantly change our view of the present and 'update' it in line with unfolding events – revising as we do so the questions we ask of the past. But for the moment at least it is widely acknowledged that we live in an age that is strikingly different in many essentials from the world as it was a generation ago – before 1980. In ordinary language, we sum up the features that have been most influential in a catch-all term: 'globalization'. Globalization is an ambiguous word. It sounds like a process, but we often use it to describe a state – the terminal point after a period of change. All the signs are that, in economic relations at least, the pace of change in the world (in the distribution of wealth and productive activity between different regions and continents) is likely to grow. But we can, nonetheless, sketch the general features of the 'globalized world' – the stage which globalization has now reached – in a recognizable form. This is the 'present' whose unpredictable making the history in this book attempts to explain.

These features can be briefly summarized as follows:

1. the appearance of a single global market – not for all but for most widely used products, and also for the supply of capital, credit and financial services;

2. the intense interaction between states that may be geographically very distant but whose interests (even in the case of very small states) have become global, not regional;

3. the deep penetration of most cultures by globally organized media, whose commercial and cultural messages (especially through the language of 'brands') have become almost inseparable;

4. the huge scale of migrations and diasporas (forced and free), creating networks and connections that rival the impact of the great European out-migration of the nineteenth century or the Atlantic slave trade;

5. the emergence from the wreck of the 'bipolar age' (1945–89) of a single 'hyperpower', whose economic and military strength, in relation to all other states, has had no parallel in modern world history;

6. the dramatic resurgence of China and India as manufacturing powers. In hugely increasing world output and shifting the balance

of the world economy, the economic mobilization of their vast populations (1.3 billion and 1 billion respectively) has been likened to the opening of vast new lands in the nineteenth century.

This list ought to provoke a series of questions. Why, in a globalized world, should one state have attained such exceptional power? Why has the economic revival of China and India been such a recent development? Why until recently have the countries of the West (now including Japan) enjoyed such a long lead in technological skills and in their standards of living? Why do the products of Westernized culture (in science, medicine, literature and the arts) still command for the most part the highest prestige? Why does the international states system, with its laws and norms, reflect the concepts and practice of European statecraft, and territorial formatting on the European model? The globalized world of the late twentieth century was not the predictable outcome of a global free market. Nor could we deduce it from the state of the world five centuries ago. It was the product of a long, confused and often violent history, of sudden reversals of fortune and unexpected defeats. Its roots stretch back (so it is widely believed) to the 'Age of Discovery' – back, indeed, to the death of Tamerlane.

Of course, there have been numerous theories and histories without number explaining and debating the course of world history. The history (and prehistory) of globalization has always been controversial. Since most of the features of globalization seemed closely related to the growth of European (later Western) predominance, it could hardly be otherwise. Among the first to imagine a globalized world were the British free-traders of the 1830s and '40s, who drew their inspiration from Adam Smith. Worldwide free trade, so they reasoned, would make war unthinkable. If every country depended upon foreign suppliers and customers, the web of mutual dependence would be too strong to break. Warrior aristocracies that thrived in a climate of conflict would become obsolete. The bourgeois ideal of representative government, spread by traders and trade, would become universal. This cheerful account of how enlightened self-interest would remake the world to the profit of all was punctured by Karl Marx. Marx insisted

that, sooner or later (he expected it to be sooner), industrial capitalism would drown its markets in goods. It could survive for a while by cutting its costs, driving wages below the cost of subsistence. But when the workers revolted – as revolt they must – capitalism would implode and the proletariat would rule. The world beyond Europe would be caught up in the struggle. In their hunger for markets, the European capitalists were bound to invade Asia (Marx's example was India) and wreck its pre-modern economies. The Indian weaver would go to the wall for the sake of Lancashire profits. India's village system and its social order were 'disappearing not so much through the brutal interference of the British tax-gatherer and ... soldier, as [through] the working of English steam and English free trade'.[4] The saving grace of this work of destruction was its unintended consequence. It would bring a social revolution to Asia, without which (so Marx implied) the rest of the world would not reach its socialist destiny.

Marx had argued that a global economy would grow out of Europe's demands. Lenin insisted that capitalism depended upon economic imperialism, and predicted its downfall in a global revolt of colonial peoples.[5] The Marx–Lenin version, half-history, half-prophecy, seemed the key to world history. From the 1920s onward it exerted huge intellectual influence. It saw Europe's economic expansion as the irresistible force ruling the rest of the world. But, instead of creating the bourgeois utopia promised by the British free-traders, it had divided the world. The capitalist-industrial zone that was centred in Europe (and its American offspring) had become richer and richer. But across the rest of the globe, colonial subjection or semi-colonial dependence brought growing impoverishment. Capitalist wealth and Europe's imperial power had combined to enforce a grossly unequal bargain. 'Free' trade had been used in the non-Western world to destroy old artisan industries, block industrial growth, and lock local economies into producing cheap raw materials. Indeed, because those raw materials would get steadily cheaper than the industrial goods for which they were meant to pay (or so ran the argument), poverty and dependence could only get worse, unless and until the 'world system' they sprang from was demolished by force.[6]

For much of the twentieth century, this pessimistic view of the motives and meaning of globalization (though the term was not used), sometimes combined with remarkable faith in its revolutionary outcome, was more than a match for the claims of the optimists who saw the result of a fully global economy as being 'modernization' (i.e. the replication of the West's social structure). Both attitudes had in common the unquestioned assumption that Europe (or the West) was the only real source of historical change. Both sides made use of the astonishing insights (and even more astonishing industry) of the great German sociologist Max Weber (1864–1920). Weber was fascinated by the peculiar trajectory that Europe had followed compared with India or China. While Marx had laid stress on the social revolution that replaced Europe's feudal society with bourgeois-ruled capitalism, Weber searched for the pattern of institutions and beliefs that had made Europe 'different'. Capitalism had developed in other parts of Eurasia, but Europe alone had made the transition to modern industrial capitalism, and the world pre-eminence that this had brought with it. At the heart of Weber's explanation was the idea that modern capitalism required above all an activist, rationalizing mentality. Chinese Confucianism (rational but inactive), Islam (active but irrational) and Hinduism (inactive and irrational) all discouraged the vital combination. 'No path led from the magical religiosity of the non-intellectual classes of Asia to a rational, methodical control of life.'[7] But European Protestantism had created (accidentally) the crucial psychology (and the institutional trappings) that allowed the breakthrough.

Weber's insistence that Europe's peculiarity must be explained in terms of a distinct socio-cultural complex inspired an enormous literature once his work became widely known (and translated) in the 1920s and after. It had a special appeal to those who rejected the crude Marxian argument that Europe's wealth and success had been gained by the plunder and pillage of the rest of the world. It encouraged the search for the critical factor(s) that had tipped the balance in Europe towards productive investment and continuous technical change. It seemed to confirm the belief (much older than Weber) that European society was uniquely dynamic, and that other great cultures, however magnificent, lacked the vital ingredients for material progress. Indeed, on this central issue, there was no real difference between the Weberian view and that taken for granted by the champions

of the Marxian 'world system'. For good or ill, from bad motives or none, Europe had energized a stationary world.

It is easy to see why in more recent years this Europe-centred account of modern world history has come under fire. The rapid dissolution of Europe's colonial empires after 1945 created a mass of new nations. Each needed a history that placed its own progress at the heart of the story. Each had its own heroes whose national struggle had been waged in the face of Europe's cultural arrogance. New 'nationalist' histories portrayed European rule (or influence) as unjust and repressive. Far from bringing progress to stationary parts of the world, European interference had blocked the social and cultural advances that were already in train. In the 1970s and '80s, 'subaltern' history dug into the fabric of many ex-colonial societies. It revealed complex peasant communities, fiercely resistant to control by outsiders, whose lives were disrupted by the clumsy if not brutal attempt to impose colonial 'order'.[8] 'Decolonized history' encouraged many different social, ethnic, religious or cultural groups to emerge from the shadows. The old colonial narratives in which Europeans stood out against the dark local backcloth now seemed like cartoons: crude and incomplete sketches of a crowded reality. The ambitions and projects of colonized peoples – teachers, writers, merchants, peasants, migrants and minorities – were described and documented. The 'stationary worlds' in which Europeans had posed as the sole 'dynamic' force were now to be seen as teeming with life. And, far from exerting a confident mastery, Europeans (in this new perspective) were often outwitted, exploited or simply ignored by locals busy with their own affairs.

This was not the first time that historians had argued that even colonized peoples had an autonomous history worthy of serious study. Before the Second World War, the young Dutch historian J. C. van Leur (1908–42) had denounced the writing of Indonesian history through European eyes – 'from the deck of the ship, the ramparts of the fortress, the high gallery of the trading house', as if nothing could happen without a European being present, or at his instigation.[9] Van Leur was killed in the war, and his ideas reached a wider international audience only in the late 1950s. But his work added a key new dimension to the historical attack on a Europe-centred world history.

It dismissed the idea that the arrival of Europeans by sea in the sixteenth century had transformed Asia's trading economy. Instead, Europeans were latecomers in a huge maritime commerce, pioneered by Asians, linking China, Japan, South East Asia, India, the Persian Gulf, the Red Sea and East Africa. Far from awaiting the Promethean touch of merchants from Europe, a 'global' economy already existed.[10] If global economic convergence was a dominant theme in modern world history, the part played by Asians (and other non-Europeans) could not be ignored. Indeed, 'globalization' – in the wider sense of the term – could no longer be seen as just a European project.

In the last twenty years, van Leur's original insight has been widened much further. The scale of global mobility, the growth of diasporas, the porous nature of frontiers, the limited power of most states, and the new distribution of industrial power (especially in Asia) have radically altered our sense of the past and what we want to know from it. For the moment at least, writing the history of nations and states seems much less important than tracing the origins of our world of movement, with its frenetic exchange of goods and ideas, its hybrid cultures and its fluid identities. A new global history has grown up in response. Its units of study are regions or oceans, long-distance trades, networks of merchants, the tracks of wandering scholars, the traffic of cults and beliefs between cultures and continents. Viewed from this level, the radical difference between Europe and Asia, the central assumption of older world histories, looks much less impressive. Instead, a chain of 'connectedness', both commercial and cultural, linked much of early modern Eurasia just at the time when (in older accounts) Europe's divergence from Asia was becoming decisive. Notions of universal empire, a new 'culture of travel', and millenarian rumours and fantasies circulated around the huge land mass between Spain and the Bay of Bengal.[11] Geographical location in Asia or Europe begins to look much less important for social and cultural change than a position astride Eurasia's trunk lines of trade, or in the arid belt where long-distance travellers did not have to toil through forest, jungle or marsh.[12]

A similar change of emphasis can be seen among historians writing the new 'global history of material progress'. As van Leur had suggested, the facile conclusion that Europeans had galvanized a somnol-

ent Asia after Vasco da Gama's arrival in India in 1498 was a travesty of the facts. A dense mercantile network already linked ports and producers between the coast of East Africa and the South China Sea. Asian merchants were not passive victims of a European takeover. Whatever their shortcomings, Asian governments were more than the predatory despots of European mythology who crushed trade and agriculture by penal taxation and arbitrary seizure. In different parts of Asia, there were market economies where the division of labour, specialized trades and urban development (the hallmarks of growth as Adam Smith had described it) looked very similar to those found in Europe. In China, especially, the scale of commercial exchange, the sophistication of credit, the use of technology, and the volume of production (in textiles particularly) revealed a pre-industrial economy at least as dynamic as contemporary Europe's. Indeed, before 1800 what really stood out was not the sharp economic contrast between Europe and Asia, but, on the contrary, a Eurasian world of 'surprising resemblances' in which a number of regions, European and Asian, were at least theoretically capable of the great leap forward into the industrial age.[13]

Meanwhile, Europe's assumed centrality in accounts of world history had come under attack from a quite different quarter. From the late 1970s, an intellectual movement inspired by the Palestinian-American Edward Said denounced the classics of European writing on the history, ethnography and culture of Asia (and by extension elsewhere) as 'orientalist' fantasy. According to Said, European description was fatally flawed by the crude attribution of stereotyped qualities, almost always demeaning, and the persistent attempt to portray Asian societies as the slothful, corrupt or degenerate antitheses of an energetic, masterful and progressive Europe.[14] A huge literary industry sprang up to pick over the language and content of the various genres that transmitted the image of the non-Western world to an audience in Europe. The implication was clear. If the Europeans' reportage (whether fact or fiction) was intended to serve the ulterior aim of extending Europe's hegemony, or even if it did so unconsciously, it had no historical value except as a reflection of Europeans' own fears and obsessions. The comparative study of Europe and non-Europe was hopelessly compromised. It could even be argued (and some writers did so) that history itself was an alien enterprise that forced knowledge of the past into the concepts and categories invented in (and for) Europe.

Few intelligent people accepted the logical conclusion of this post-modern extremism – that nothing could be known and that all inquiry was hopeless. But the broader point held good: that European depic-tions of other parts of the world needed very careful decoding. The Saidian critique was part of a great sea change, a conscious attempt to 'decentre' Europe or even to 'provincialize' it. European accounts of other cultures and peoples should no longer be treated as the 'authorized version', however full or persuasive. Europe should no longer be seen as the pivot of change, or as the agent acting on the passive civilizations of the non-Western world. Above all, perhaps, the European path to the modern world should no longer be treated as natural or 'normal', the standard against which historical change in other parts of the world should always be measured. Europeans had forged their own kind of modernity, but there were other mod-ernities – indeed, many modernities.[15]

RETHINKING THE HISTORY OF EUROPE'S EXPANSION

'Decolonized history' has cut Europe down to size. It has made it much harder to assume unthinkingly that European societies were inherently progressive, or that they were necessarily more efficient than other peoples in Eurasia – or on other continents. European definitions of 'progress', like European observations on the rest of the world, have lost their once unchallenged authority. Indeed, some modern writers reject the validity of any comparison between different cultures (because no one can be an insider in more than one culture), in the curious belief that a much-jumbled world is really composed of distinct and original cultures. Post-colonial history takes a generally sceptical view of the European impact and an even more sceptical view of the 'improvements' once claimed for colonial rule. It treats 'colonial' history as myopic and biased, perhaps even delusory, and its claims as so much propaganda aimed at opinion at home. Indeed,

closer inspection has suggested an ironic reversal of the colonialist case. Far from dragging backward peoples towards European-style modernity, colonial rule was more likely to impose a form of 'anti-modernity'. Caste in India symbolized Indian backwardness. Yet British rulers, for their own convenience, struck a bargain with Brahmins to harden caste status into an administrative system (for-malized in the census).[16] In colonial Africa a parallel process took place as clans and followings were reinvented as 'tribes', with chiefly rulers as their ancestral leaders.[17] Here, as in India, a political gambit was carefully packaged as an act of respect to local tradition. In the colonial version of history, caste and tribe were inscribed as imme-morial features of the Indian and African past. In imperial propa-ganda, they became the genetic flaws that made self-rule for Indians and Africans impossible. But in 'decolonized history' the expansion of Europe appears as a vast conspiracy to reorder the non-Western world along pseudo-traditional lines, the better to hold it in check and exploit its resources – indefinitely.

On these and other grounds, Europe's place in world history now looks rather different from that in conventional accounts written a few decades ago. But histories that aim to 'provincialize' Europe still leave a lot to explain. The European states were the main force that created the 'globalized' world of the late nineteenth century. They were the chief authors of the two great transformations that were locked together in the 'modern world' of the 1870s to the 1940s. The first was the making of a world economy not just of long-distance trade in high-value luxuries but of the global exchange of manufactures, raw materials and foodstuffs, in huge volumes and values, with the accompanying flows of people and money. This was an economic revolution that was chiefly managed (not always well) from Europe or by Europeans, and fashioned to suit their particular interests. The second transformation was closely connected. This was the extension of European rule, overt and covert, across huge swathes of the non-European world – a process under way before 1800, but accelerating sharply in the nineteenth century. It was strikingly visible in the colo-nial partitions of Africa, South East Asia, the South Pacific and (later) the Middle East; in the great ventures of empire-building in North Asia (by Russia) and South Asia (by Britain); in the subjection of much of maritime China to foreign controls; and in the European occupation (by demographic imperialism) of the Americas, Australasia and parts of South Central Africa. In Africa, the Middle East, much of South East Asia, the Pacific, Australasia and even the Americas, it created the territorial units that provide the state structure of the contemporary world.

Europe thus engaged in a double expansion. The outward signs of the first were the spread of railways and steamships, building a vast web of connections much faster and more certain than in earlier times and capable of pouring a huge stream of goods into once inaccessible places. Harbour works, railway stations, telegraph lines, warehouses, banks, insurance companies, shops, hotels (like Shepheards' in Cairo or Raffles' in Singapore), clubs and even churches formed the global grid of Europe's commercial empire, allowing free passage to European merchants and trade and easing their access to a mass of new customers. The second mode was territorial. It meant the acquisition of forts and bases from which soldiers and warships could be sent to coerce or conquer. It meant the control of key zones astride the maritime highways that ran between Europe and the rest of the world: the classic case was Egypt, occupied by Britain in 1882. It meant a pattern of rule through which the products and revenues of colonial regions could be diverted at will to imperial purposes. Once their Raj was in place, the British taxed Indians to pay for the military power – a sepoy army – that they needed in Asia. Europe's commercial empire and its territorial empires did not overlap completely. But the crucial point about this double expansion was its interdependence. Territorial imperialism was a battering ram. It could break open markets that resisted free trade, or (as in India) conscript local resources to build the railways and roads that European traders demanded. It could promise protection to European entrepreneurs, or (as happened often in Africa) make them a free gift of local land and labour. But it also relied on the technological, industrial and financial assets that Europe could deploy. These might be decisive when it came to fighting – steam-powered ships and superior weaponry helped win Britain's first war in China in 1839–42 – though certainly not in all places.[18] The real advantage of industrial imperialism lay in scale and speed. Industrial technique and the supply of capital allowed

Europeans to stage a series of blitzkrieg conquests. They could lay down railways at breakneck speed to bring their force to bear hundreds of miles from the sea. They could flood a new zone with European settlers and transform its demography almost overnight, disorienting indigenous peoples and making resistance seem futile. They could transform alien environments with amazing completeness into a familiar European-style habitat: introducing wild animals, birds, fish, trees and flowers as well as crops and livestock. Above all, they could turn even the remotest parts of the globe into suppliers of the everyday goods like butter, meat or cheese once reserved for local producers at home. The gaunt freezing works with their grimy smokestacks that sprang up round the coasts of New Zealand after 1880 were the industrial face of colonization.

It would be wrong to suppose that Europeans lacked the support of allies and helpers; but they played the critical role in remaking the world. But how do we explain the extraordinary shift, which seemed all but complete by 1914, from a world of Eurasian 'connectedness' to a global-imperial world? Despite the libraries of writing that deal with the subject, much remains puzzling. Those magical dates 1492 (when Columbus crossed the Atlantic) and 1498 (when Vasco da Gama arrived in India) may have signalled the start of Europe's new era. But the pace of advance was spasmodic at best. Three centuries after Columbus had made landfall, most of the North American mainland remained unoccupied and virtually unexplored by Europeans. It took nearly three hundred years for the corner of India where Vasco da Gama had landed to fall under European rule (Calicut was annexed by the British in 1792). The rush started only at the turn of the nineteenth century. Not just the timing, but the form and direction of Europe's expansion need more explanation. Why did the Ottoman Empire and Iran preserve their autonomy long after India, which was much further away? Why was India subjected to colonial rule while China was able to keep its sovereign status, though much hedged about, and Japan had become a colonial power by 1914? If industrial capitalism was the key to the spread of European influence, why did its impact take so long to be felt across so much of the world, and with such variable consequences? Why were Europe's own divisions, periodically unleashed with such lethal effect, not more destructive of its imperial ambitions? And what indeed should be counted as 'non-Europe'? Why did some parts of 'non-Europe' succeed so much better than others at keeping Europe at bay, or throw off its grip more quickly? And how much was left, once Europe's empires collapsed, of the 'world Europe had made'?

To answer these questions, it seems wise to adopt a somewhat different approach from that of previous histories. Four basic assumptions have shaped the arguments advanced in this book. The first is that we should reject the idea of a linear change in the course of modern world history, in which Europe *progressively* rose to preeminence, then fell and rose again as part of the 'West'. It is more productive to think in terms of 'conjunctures', periods of time when certain general conditions in different parts of the world coincided to encourage (or check) the enlargement of trade, the expansion of empires, the exchange of ideas or the movement of people. The way that this happened might tilt the balance of advantage between different parts of the world, temporarily at least. One condition alone was rarely decisive. Producers and consumers might wish to do business. But governments and rulers also had to agree to permit free(ish) trade – or any trade at all. Politics and geopolitics were a vital part of the equation. The outbreak of wars and their unpredictable course could shatter one equilibrium and impose another. Thus the great expansion of trade in the late nineteenth century and the kinds of globalization it helped to promote came to a shuddering halt with the First World War. After 1929, 'deglobalization' set in with catastrophic results. Europe's original breakthrough to a position of primacy in its global relations is much better seen as the unexpected result of a revolution in Eurasia than as the outcome of a steady advance in Columbus's footsteps. The appropriate imagery is not of rivers or tides, but of earthquakes and floods.

The second assumption is that we must set Europe's age of expansion firmly in its Eurasian context. That means recognizing the *central* importance of Europe's connections with other Old World civilizations and states in Asia, North Africa and the Middle East. Of course, Europe's forced entry into the 'Outer World' and the 'neo-Europes' it created in the Americas, Australasia and Southern Africa were a key part of the story. Without the exploitation of American resources,

and the commercial integration of North East America and North West Europe to form an 'Atlantic' economy, the eventual creation of a global economy in the late nineteenth century might not have happened at all. But the staggering scale of American wealth – the wonder of the world for more than a century – should not distract us. The centre of gravity in modern world history lies in Eurasia – in the troubled, conflicted, connected and intimate relations of its great cultures and states, strung out in a line from the European 'Far West' to the Asian 'Far East'.

Perhaps surprisingly, the most forceful statement of this 'Eurasian' view was made a century ago by a British geographer-imperialist, Halford Mackinder.[19] Mackinder was keen to remind his audience that the 'Columbian epoch', when European sea power had seemed to master the world, was only an interlude. The advantage of sea over land as a means of travel was temporary, not permanent: the invention of railways had seen to that. Before long the dominant influence in the world's affairs would revert to the power(s) that commanded Eurasia (what Mackinder called the 'world island') by controlling its 'heartland'. From this central position, and with a network of railways to mobilize vast resources, a Eurasian empire could drive any rival to the world's maritime fringe – the 'Outer World' of the Americas, sub-Saharan Africa, island South East Asia and Oceania – and even challenge it there. There is no need to follow Mackinder's geopolitical vision to its logical end (his aim after all was to puncture the complacency of the Edwardian Establishment), although the nightmare scenario of a 'heartland' super-empire became less far-fetched in the age of Nazi and Soviet imperialism. What we can see today, perhaps even more clearly than he, is that the shifting balance of wealth and power between Eurasia's main elements, and the different terms on which these elements entered the global economy and the modern 'world system', form the hammer and anvil of modern world history.

It might even be argued that Europe's annexation of the Outer World is only a part of this Eurasian history, and depended heavily upon Eurasian developments. In sub-Saharan Africa and in South East Asia, Europeans found themselves in competition with other Old World empires and their client states. After c.1870, fear of a 'peaceful invasion' by Chinese and Japanese settlers created racial paranoia all round the 'white' Pacific, in Australia, New Zealand and on the Pacific coast of North America. But it was also true that European efforts to create viable colonies in Outer World regions depended on co-opting or conscripting the resources of non-European Eurasia. India's taxes, soldiers, merchants and manpower (often in the form of indentured labour) helped throw open East Africa, parts of mainland South East Asia and the island Pacific as far away as Fiji to European (in this case British) enterprise. Chinese traders, miners and artisans were just as important in what became British Malaya and the Dutch East Indies (modern Indonesia). The critical fact was that Chinese and Indians came not as the agents of a Chinese or Indian expansion, but as the auxiliaries and accessories of one directed from Europe.

The third assumption is that we need to think out very carefully what that 'Europe' was. There are obvious objections to treating Europe as a unity when it was at best a loose and quarrelsome 'commonwealth'. Thus when we talk about 'European primacy', what we really mean is the collective primacy of the European states, especially those most active in overseas trade and empire. Part of the difficulty is that the word 'Europe' has acquired at least three different meanings: a geographical space; a socio-political community; and a cultural programme.[20] An easy solution, in writing of Europe's global expansion, has been to treat the continent's north-west corner as its centre of power. Britain, the Low Countries, northern France and western Germany become the 'quintessence' of Europe, setting the 'European' standard of economic and cultural modernity. Explaining Europe's successes is then a straightforward matter of invoking the strength and efficiency of its representative 'core states'.

In any long view of Europe's place in Eurasia (or in global history) this reductive approach is very misleading – for three different reasons. Firstly, the north-western states were not free agents who could disregard events in the rest of the continent – even after they had become Europe's richest section. Their wealth and safety were always dependent on the general stability of the European 'states system'. Turmoil in Central or Eastern Europe, or a major disturbance in the overall balance of power, could threaten their sovereignty or bring them windfall gains – in Europe or beyond. In fact in the period covered by this book no part of Europe achieved a lasting supremacy over all the

others. The commercial prosperity of the north-western states was balanced by the military and demographic weight of the empires further east. The Europe of nations (in the west) might look down its nose at the Europe of empires (in the east), but it had to live with it. Coexistence was often explosive. The quarrels and conflicts of the European states, reaching a terrible climax in the twentieth century, were a constant limiting factor on their collective ability to impose Europe's domination on the rest of the world.

Secondly, too narrow a view of what Europe was ignores the problem of Russia. A long liberal tradition took a sceptical view of Russia's European credentials, seeing tsarist Russia as an 'Asiatic despotism', too crude and too poor to be 'one of us'. Some Russian thinkers returned the compliment by insisting that Russia was a separate (and superior) civilization untainted by Europe's amoral industrialism. A realistic view would see Russia, like Spain or the Habsburg Empire, as one of the frontier states that played a vanguard role in Europe's expansion.[21] The eventual predominance of the West European states across much of Southern Asia after 1815 was really achieved in a fractious involuntary partnership with Russia. Russia's huge inland empire, pivoted around Inner Asia, gradually absorbed much of the North Asian land mass. Ottomans, Iranians, Chinese and Japanese faced the British and French with Russia closing in behind them. The vast (but incomplete) encirclement of Asia by Europe was the great geopolitical fact of the nineteenth-century world. But, for all the pedantry of liberals and Slavophiles, the 'power supply' behind Russia's expansion was in fact its European identity: the leverage granted by its first-class membership of the European states system; the economic energy that flowed from Russia's integration into the European economy; and the intellectual access that Russians enjoyed, from the sixteenth century onward, to the general pool of European ideas and culture. Russians, like other Europeans, claimed their conquests as a 'civilizing mission'.

Thirdly, there is a powerful case for broadening our notion of 'Europe' to the west as well as the east. The importance of the Atlantic economy has already been mentioned. A vast economic space that included the West African coast, the Caribbean islands, the North American seaboard, Mexico, Peru and maritime Brazil was annexed to Europe commercially after 1500. The precise contribution of this mainly slave-labour zone to Europe's later industrialization has remained controversial, and may not have been large.[22] But the important point is that by the early nineteenth century, and perhaps even before, a significant part of this Atlantic world can no longer be seen as Europe's dependent periphery. The 'Old Northeast' of the United States, with its metropolis in New York, was functionally part of Europe's leading commercial region. It was an active – and became the dominant – partner in developing the agrarian lands in the American South and Midwest, its inland empire. By the 1870s it was financially and industrially on a par with Europe's richest countries. Although America's separate identity was loudly proclaimed by its politicians and writers, and fear of involvement in European quarrels ruled its diplomacy, America's relations with Europe were not cold or detached. Between the Old Northeast and North West Europe, the traffic of goods, technology, ideas and people was extremely dense. In culture and technology it was a two-way movement, with a strong mutual influence. By fits and starts, with retreats and advances, Old Europe and New Europe were being subsumed into a larger formation, the 'West'. It was a volatile process, on which the peculiar trajectory of American capitalism – with its huge corporate scale and aggressive protectionism – had a powerful impact. But it was one of the keys to Europe's place in Eurasia, and to both the duration and the mutation of Europe's leading place in the world.

The fourth assumption concerns our understanding of empire. Empire is often seen as the original sin of European peoples, who corrupted an innocent world. Of course its real origins are much older, and lie in a process almost universal in human societies. It was a human characteristic, remarked Adam Smith in *The Wealth of Nations* (1776), to want to 'truck, barter and exchange'.[23] Smith was thinking of material goods: it was the habit of exchange that allowed the division of labour, the real foundation of economic life. But he might well have extended his philosophical insight to the parallel world of information and ideas. The exchange of information, knowledge, beliefs and ideas – sometimes over enormous distances – has been just as typical of human societies as the eagerness to acquire useful, prestigious or exotic goods by purchase or barter. Both kinds

of exchange bring consequences with them. A supply of cheap firearms (to take an obvious example) could shift the balance of power inside a society where firearms were scarce or unknown with astonishing speed, and unleash a huge cycle of violence against humans or nature. The spread of Christianity and Islam transformed their converts' conception of their place in the world, and their notions of loyalty to neighbours and rulers. As these cases suggest, at all times in history the exchange of goods and ideas has upset the cohesion of some societies much more than others, making them vulnerable to internal breakdown, and to takeover by outsiders. So a second propensity in human communities has been the accumulation of power on an extensive scale: the building of empires. Indeed, the difficulty of forming autonomous states on an ethnic basis, against the gravitational pull of cultural or economic attraction (as well as disparities of military force), has been so great that empire (where different ethnic communities fall under a common ruler) has been the default mode of political organization throughout most of history. Imperial power has usually been the rule of the road.

But if empire is 'normal', why has its practice by Europeans aroused such passionate hostility – a hostility still strongly reflected in most of what is written on the subject? Part of the answer is that so many post-colonial states found it natural to base their political legitimacy on the rejection of empire as an alien, evil and oppressive force. Some forty years on, this tradition is stronger than ever. Part of the reason is the far wider exposure to European empire-building than to that of (for example) the Mongols, the Ottoman Turks or the Chinese in Inner Asia. The constituency of the aggrieved is thus much larger. But the intensity of feeling also reflects the belief (expressed in much of the historical writing) that there was something qualitatively different about the empires that the Europeans made. Unlike the traditional agrarian empires that merely accumulated land and people, the arch-characteristic of European imperialism was expropriation. Land was expropriated to meet the needs of plantations and mines engaged in long-distance commerce. Slave labour was acquired and carried thousands of miles to serve the same purpose. Native peoples were displaced, and their property rights nullified, on the grounds that they had failed to make proper use of their land. Both native peoples and slaves (by different forms of displacement) suffered the effective expropriation of their cultures and identities: they were reduced to fragments, without hope of recovering the worlds they had lost. They became peoples without a history. And where expropriation by subjugation proved insufficient, European colonizers turned to their ultimate remedies: exclusion, expulsion or liquidation. 'If we reason from what passes in the world,' wrote the French thinker de Tocqueville in 1835, after a visit to America, 'we should almost say that the European is to the other races of mankind what man himself is to the lower animals: he makes them subservient to his use, and when he cannot subdue he destroys them.'[24]

This chilling account of the European version of empire (as practised outside Europe) seemed amply confirmed by what took place in the New World of the Americas, where Europeans (for reasons discussed in Chapter 2) were much freer than elsewhere to impose their will.

Until c.1800 it looked as if a variety of factors would prevent a similar pattern in other parts of the world. Distance, disease and demography would sustain much more determined resistance. Even where Europeans had established their bridgeheads, they would be forced to 'creolize' and make social and cultural peace with Afro-Asian peoples. But this is not what happened. In the nineteenth century, Europe's expansion was supercharged by technological and cultural change. Europe's capacity to intrude and interfere was transformed on two levels. Europeans acquired the means to assert their will on the ground – by force if necessary – over far more of the world. Most spectacularly in India, they imposed their rule directly on the conquered population, taxing, policing and laying down the law. At the same time, the growth of a Europe-centred international economy, the extension of a Europe-centred international system with its own laws and norms, and the spread of European ideas via Europe-owned media (like the telegraph, mail and steamship services) created a new environment at the 'macro' level. Europeans, it seemed, controlled all the lines of communication. Above the very local level, nothing could move unless it adapted to their ways. Trapped between these upper and nether millstones, it is hardly surprising that colonized peoples in Asia and Africa should have likened their condition to that of the Europeans' first victims in the Americas.

We shall see later on why this was too pessimistic, in some cases at least. Even supercharged Europe needed local cooperation, and had to pay its price. Some of what it offered was quickly adapted for local 'self-strengthening', building up the local capacity to build states and cultures. Some of it chimed with the aims of local reformers. Some of the claims of colonialism's fiercest antagonists now look less patriotic and more like the outcry of privilege displaced. Nevertheless, it seems unlikely that we will be able to take a detached and apolitical view of Europe's empire-building for a long time to come. In too much of the world its effects are too recent to be allowed to slip into the 'past' – that zone of time whose events we regard as having only an indirect influence on our own affairs. It may be an age before we regard it more coolly as a phase in world history – perhaps an inevitable phase – rather than as the result of the moral and cultural aggression of one part of the world.

There is one final complication that we may need to unravel. It is commonplace to talk of the 'modern' world, to describe the changes that made it as 'modernization', and to treat the attainment of 'modernity' as the most critical change in the history of a state or community. The intermeshing processes that we call globalization are usually thought of as part of modernity, since 'modern' societies supposedly interact more intensely with each other than did their 'pre-modern' counterparts. Modernization thus has a close and uncomfortable affinity with the expansion of Europe.

But modernity is a very slippery idea. The conventional meaning is based on a scale of achievement. In political terms, its key attributes are an organized nation state, with definite boundaries; an orderly government, with a loyal bureaucracy to carry out its commands; an effective means to represent public opinion; and a code of rights to protect the ordinary citizen and encourage the growth of 'civil society'. Economically, it means the attainment of rapid, cumulative economic growth through industrial capitalism (with its social and technological infrastructure); the entrenchment of individual property rights (as a necessary precondition); and the systematic exploitation of science-based knowledge. Culturally, it implies the separation of religion and the supernatural from the mainstream of thought (by secularization and the 'disenchantment' of knowledge) and social behaviour; the diffusion of literacy (usually through a vernacular rather than a classical language); and a sense of common origins and identity (often based on language) within a 'national' community. The keynotes of modernity become order, discipline, hierarchy and control in societies bent on purposeful change towards ever higher levels of 'social efficiency'.

It is easy to see that most of these criteria are really a description of what was supposed to have happened in Europe. Europe became modern; non-Europe stayed pre-modern – until modernized by Europe. The result is often a crude dichotomy that sees Europeans as the invariable agents of progress in a world elsewhere glued to 'tradition'. We have seen already that this view is hard to defend. There are three other difficulties. First, the elements of modernity (as listed above) were rarely all present in a single society. In much of Europe they were barely visible until very recent times. Even those countries that we think of as pioneers of modernity had strong pre-modern features. Slavery was lawful in the United States until 1863. The ruling class of Victorian Britain was largely chosen by birth, and religion remained central to social aspiration and identity. Twentieth-century America was a caste society whose marker was colour, used to exclude a large social fragment from civil and political rights until the 1960s or later. Post-revolutionary France confined the Rights of Man to men until 1945, when women gained the vote. Viewed from this angle, the threshold for modernity becomes very uncertain. Was Nazi Germany modern, or Soviet Russia? Are there objective tests for modernity, or is 'modern' simply a label for regimes we approve of? Second, some of the key features of conventional modernity were also to be found in parts of Eurasia far away from Europe. The classic case is China, which developed a 'modern' bureaucracy selected on merit, a commercial economy and a technological culture long before Europe. Was China modern, with some pre-modern survivals, or the other way round? Nor was Western-style modernity eventually taken up in the non-Western world without many local adjustments. How are these to be seen? Is there one modernity, or are there 'many modernities'?[25] Third, it may be the case, as the example of China suggests, that other kinds of modernity were not doomed to failure because their flaws were inherent. Instead it seems possible (some would say obvious)

that Europe's expansion amounted in part to a deliberate assault on the modernizing ventures of other peoples and states. Perhaps it was not Europe's modernity that triumphed, but its superior capacity for organized violence.

Modernity is too useful an idea to be thrown away. But it may be wise to accept it as a fuzzy abstraction – as a rough-and-ready checklist of the social and cultural patterns that favoured the production of wealth and power at a particular time. For the term to be helpful, however, it ought to throw light on the relative success of different communities caught up in the greater regional and global connectedness that accelerated so sharply after the mid eighteenth century. Being modern was not an absolute state, but a comparative one – indeed a competitive one. The best test of modernity might be the extent to which, in any given society, resources and people could be mobilized for a task, and redeployed continuously as new needs arose or new pressures were felt. In principle, many different societies possessed this ability. In practice, and for reasons that we are far from understanding fully, for almost two centuries after 1750 it was North West European societies (and their transatlantic offspring) that mobilized fastest and also coped best with the social and political strains that being mobile imposed. Far-flung empires, and a global economy shaped to their interests, were to be their reward.

Guide to Reading Peter Perdue's Chapter "Writing the National Histories"
and parts of his Chapter "State Building in Europe and Asia" from *China
Marches West*

These selections are taken from a long and detailed account of how the Qing
emperors conquered a part of what Perdue calls Central Eurasia. The events,
leading figures, and even the regions will probably be unknown to you. That
means that names of people and places will add to the challenge of
assimilating the essential information. Do not be intimidated by the details
but search for Perdue's leading arguments. Think about how some history is
written in overt service of a regime. Think of these readings as a soul-
searching conversation that Perdue is having with nationalist historians in
Russia, China, and Mongolia. He is also addressing historians in the West.

1. Locate Central Eurasia on a web site, using some of the names of the
peoples and places of the region. Have any parts of the region been in the
news in recent years and if so why?

2. You have discussed "agency" in an earlier tutorial. How do you think the
concept applies to these readings?

3. China under the later Qing (nineteenth century) is occasionally
represented as a weak victim of European imperialism and there are good
reasons for that depiction. However, Perdue offers a more complicated
assessment. What is it?

4. Can you see some connections between these readings and that of John
Darwin?

5. Perdue wants serious and truthful scholars to avoid the simplistic
generalizations of theory or narratives written for nationalistic purposes. In
their place, he proposes what guidelines?

6. The second of the readings suggests that instead of contrasting European
and Chinese Empires, we must try to think of themes that are more of less
common to all. List some of these common themes. Think in terms of the
paradoxical idea of features that are the same but different.

Library of Congress Cataloging-in-Publication Data

Perdue, Peter C.
China marches west : the Qing conquest of Central Eurasia / Peter C. Perdue.
p. cm.
Includes bibliographical references and index.
ISBN 0-674-01684-x (alk. paper)
1. China—History—Qing dynasty, 1644-1912. 2. Russia—History—1613-1917.
3. Mongols—History. I. Title: Qing conquest of Central Eurasia. II. Title.

DS754.P47 2005
951'.03—dc22 2004059472

14

Writing the National
History of Conquest

FROM the seventeenth through the nineteenth centuries, Western and Chinese historians' views of the Qing frontier converged upon a common geopolitical perspective. Although they gave divergent evaluations of the soundness of the dynasty and its policies, they came to agree that China was a powerful entity in eastern Eurasia, one whose autonomy was vital to global security. Imperialists and nationalists were secret sharers, especially in their analysis of the future of the Qing frontiers.

Statecraft Writers and Empire

The statecraft writers Wei Yuan (1794–1856) and Gong Zizhen (1792–1841) built on the achievements of the eighteenth century to support their arguments for strong national defense. Both used history to defend the heavy cost of frontier conquest. They placed Qianlong's campaigns in a lineage reaching back to Han dynasty relations with the Xiongnu, claiming that he had successfully resolved the nearly two-millennia-long issue of securing the northwest frontier. China's borders were now stable, but the empire needed to invest in integrating the frontier regions with the interior. Like the emperor's official historians, they saw Heaven's will manifest in these unprecedented imperial victories, but like Qishiyi, they knew that a wide world existed beyond the frontiers. Carrying on the eighteenth-century project into the nineteenth-century world of international geopolitics, these writers defined the framework within which the Qing in its last century would attempt to maintain control over its conquered peoples.

Gong Zizhen and Wei Yuan are best known to Western scholars as advocates of resistance to Western maritime incursions, and of extending China's knowledge of European nations.[1] Philip Kuhn has recently pointed out, however, that "ethnocentric" Western scholars tend to exaggerate foreign influence on thinkers like Wei Yuan, ignoring his primary focus on do-

The scholar and historian Wei Yuan (1794–1856).

mestic reform.[2] Wei and Gong derived the primary impulse of their reformism from the activist "New Text" school of interpretation, which viewed classical texts as guides to action, not dusty objects of empirical research. We should not, however, view Wei and Gong solely as advocates of internal reform, nor should we stress only their concerns about maritime defense. As proponents of political activism derived from classical scholarship, Wei and Gong also closely linked security issues to domestic political reform. Security for the state meant both defense of its boundaries and maintenance of internal order. In their thinking, continental and maritime security concerns were closely tied together.

Gong Zizhen was twenty-nine years old when he wrote his prophetic essay arguing that Turkestan should be made into a province.[3] He had obtained his juren degree but failed his jinshi examination. Unsurprisingly, the little-known scholar's arguments were ignored when first published in 1820, but they received much wider attention when reprinted in the volume sponsored by the influential official He Changling and compiled by Wei Yuan, the Huangchao jingshi Wenbian (Collected imperial essays on Statecraft), in 1827. The Jahangir rebellion of 1826 had drawn attention to Turkestan's unstable situation, and the costs of maintaining garrisons in the region drew substantial criticism. Gong not only argued strongly for the benefits of incorporating the region into the empire but also justified its conquest as the culmination of a long-standing imperial vision supported by Heaven.

Unlike the Qianlong emperor, however, Gong located China not in the center of the civilized realm but at the eastern end of the Eurasian continent. It was a land with fixed borders and a defined territory. It was the largest country in the world, whose borders stretched to the four "seas," for the Qing's continental border represented the ultimate limit of control, just like the coastlines of the east and south: "Whether by land, or by sea, large or small mountains, large and small rivers, or plains, our territory is either registered land or it is like the seas." China's rulers had expanded first to the east, then to the south coast, but by dominating the Mongols, the Qing had made the northwest safe and no longer remote or dangerous. "Was it not Heavenly fate that the empire should reach to the Four Seas? Even using tens of millions of tacls cannot be called wasteful." Gong rejected the "shallow views of ignorant weaklings and vile writers" (yuru, pisheng) who said that supporting the conquest was "wasting the resources of the interior to support the frontier" (haozhong shibian).[4]

Gong also forcefully argued for integrating the region with the interior. All the landless, roaming populations of northwest and North China should be sent west, supported with twenty-year tax exemptions and funding for land clearance, while the resident garrisons should give their land to the soldiers as private property. The banners would be eliminated, and civil administrators would take control of all land and tax collection. The region would be systematically divided into prefectures and sub-prefectures, Chinese names would replace the native ones, and the *begs, jasaks,* and other frontier authorities would come under the regular administration.

Gong's radical proposals extended existing trends to their ultimate consequences. Eighteenth-century Qing policies had already promoted immigration into the new territories and created a hybrid civil and military administrative structure, but the Manchu rulers kept Turkestan separate from the rest of the empire and continued to insist that it should pay for its own support. Gong rejected the idea of self-sufficiency, arguing that the new province, like Guizhou and other poor interior regions, could receive substantial subventions from wealthier provinces. Trade, however, would be carefully controlled, so that corrupting "luxuries" could not enter: an official at the Jiayuguan gate would ensure that only grain, cloth, tea, and other essentials could enter the border region, and only melons and hides could be imported from there. In Gong's view, the Han Chinese population could make a new start here, uncontaminated by the social tension and commercial seductions of the interior. Even the exiled criminals in the region and other "wicked people" from the interior could redeem themselves there by working hard on their own lands. Gong's vision of pure virgin soil, the culmination of the extension of culture outward from the imperial center, answered his critics in moral and historical terms.

Wei Yuan supported his colleague in more material terms, stressing what James Millward calls the "forward defense dividend": transferring troops to the frontier relieved the interior provinces of the expense of supporting them at home.[5] In his essay in the *Huangchao Jingshi Wenbian,* Wei likewise praised the empire's extension in all directions, and carefully surveyed all of the people under its control.[6] The Mongols of Inner Mongolia, plus the Tumed and Guihua Mongols, comprised a total of fifty-one banners, each with its own *jasak,* divided into twenty-five tribes. The Outer Mongols formed four tribes and eighty-one banners, collectively known as Khalkha. Farther west were the towns of Zungharia, which had become large settlements after the end of the wars. (Wei did not mention the elimination of the Zunghars.) Beyond them were the "western dependent states," divided into three circuits (*lu*), which included the Kazakhs, Burut (Kirghiz), Andijanis, Afghans, Hindustanis, and others. In Wei's expansive gaze, all these peoples "belonged" (*shu*) to the empire in some sense; only Russia was not a dependent state.

He also had to defend imperial control against the charge of wasting in-

terror resources on barren wastelands. Citing the constant damage caused by nomadic raids in the past, Wei argued that the cost of frontier expansion was fully justified and, furthermore, the region could relieve population pressure in the interior. "Heaven has left us this vast wilderness," he exclaimed, to accommodate the floating population of the "flourishing age."[7]

Because Wei and Gong shared a belief in a cosmic force directing the course of history, Western analysts have often seen them as anticipating the unilinear schemes of historical analysis characteristic of nineteenth-century social theory.[8] They derived their progressivist stance, however, not from Western examples but from what they knew of the Qing's expansion. The eighteenth-century expansion seemed to demonstrate conclusively that China had fulfilled its historical destiny by dominating Central Eurasia. Just like imperialists in the New World and elsewhere, they promoted the filling up of "virgin lands" with immigrants from the core, and the tighter links to the interior, as "manifest destiny" for this large continental state. Material benefits complemented an underlying view of historical change, dependent on assumptions about the natural boundaries of the state derived from the Qing's flourishing age.

Wei Yuan's *Shengwuji* (Record of sacred military campaigns) completed the legitimation of the Qing conquests by synthesizing them into an accessible form. Born in 1794, he grew up during a time of incessant warfare when the empire was desperately fending off internal rebellion and foreign attack. As he noted in the preface, he was born one year before the Mao rebellion of 1795, received his licentiate degree when the White Lotus rebellion was suppressed, attained his first advanced degree after the attack of Lin Qing on the capital in 1814, and gained his *juren* degree during Jahangir's rebellion in Xinjiang of 1822–1828.[9] During the Opium War he served as a clerk in the office of the Liangjiang Governor-General, where he observed China's humiliating loss to the "sea barbarians." In 1842 he used the "sea of documents" available to him, including vast quantities of materials collected in the imperial campaign histories, secret official documents, private writings, and oral information, to create a comprehensive account of the Qing's military achievements that would instruct later generations, the *Shengwuji.* The *Haiguo Tuzhi,* his geography of foreign nations, appeared in 1844. Both works became extremely influential in Japan in the 1850s, just as foreign powers arrived to demand Japan's opening to trade.[10]

Wei Yuan had been anticipated by the Han official Zhao Yi, who as a secretary of the Grand Council wrote many of the communications to the northwest during the Turkestan campaigns, served on the southwest frontier for much of his life, and helped to compile the *Pingding Zhungar Fanglue.* His *Glorious Record of the Imperial Dynasty's Military Accom-*

plishments (Huangchao Wugong Jisheng), published in 1792, bridged the imperial historiographic projects of Qianlong and the private accounts of Wei Yuan and his successors. He discussed seven Qing campaigns, including two, in Burma and Taiwan, in which he had personally participated. Zhao Yi shared Wei Yuan's interest in both military history and the historical evolution of imperial institutions. He also wrote important essays analyzing the rise of the Grand Council and Hanlin Academy. In contrast to Gu Yanwu, for example, who praised the localism of ancient feudalism, Zhao Yi joined the Song tradition of "historical analogists" with the statecraft concerns of the Qing to affirm military expansion and centralized authority. Zhao Yi did not write his history out of anxieties over domestic upheaval and foreign incursions, but he prepared the way for Wei Yuan with historiography that "stressed the role of environment and continuous, cumulative institutional change, instead of looking back to a static and absolute utopian antiquity."[11]

In the preface to the *Shengwuji*, Wei offers a lengthy defense, filled with classical references, of the radical proposition that "fighting war is superior to worshipping at ancestral temples" (*zhan shengyu miaotang*). In other words, defense of secure borders should take precedence over spreading civilized culture throughout the world; ethical universalism must yield to national security. Yet Wei Yuan also stresses the superiority of "human talent" (*rencai*) over material means (*caiyong*). To ensure security, material factors cannot replace psychological factors:

If material resources (*caiyong*) are insufficient, the state will not be poor, but if human talent (*rencai*) is not dynamic (*yong*), then it will be poor. If commands do not extend beyond the seas, the state is not weak; but if commands do not extend up to the interior borders, the state is weak. So the former kings did not worry about material resources but only about talent. They did not worry that they could not exert their will over the four barbarians, but worried about exerting their will within the four borders. If all officials have ability, the state will be orderly and rich; if all within the borders obey commands, the state will be powerful.[12]

Wei clearly accepted the delimiting of borders achieved by imperial expansion and, like Gong, focused his efforts on strengthening control within them. The state's goal was not to promote culture beyond its borders but to ensure obedience within them. Here we have crossed the blurred boundary separating nationalist ideology from classical norms. For Wei, internal security depends on mobilizing the best men of the empire to compete actively (*ying*), as in battle, to defend it.

Wei derived this proto-militarist ideology primarily from the historical record of Qing conquests, not from his knowledge of Western powers. As Jane Leonard has argued, Wei's interest in foreign countries derived primarily from the classical geographical tradition.[13] Although foreign ideas made some contribution, the classical tradition and its official history contained enough intellectual material to support all three of Wei Yuan's most striking proposals: military defense, global geographic knowledge, and public participation in state affairs.

In its organization the *Shengwuji* follows the expansion of the Qing state. After the opening two *juan* on the founding of the Qing and the suppression of the Three Feudatories, Wei Yuan discusses the Zunghar campaigns as part of his treatment of the pacification of Mongolia. He organizes his account geographically, proceeding from the "Inner Six" Mongolian tribes to the "Outer Four," Kokonor, Helanshan Eleuths, and finally Kangxi's Zunghar campaigns. Successive chapters follow the imperial armies into Zungharia, Turkestan, Tibet, the Gurkha region of Nepal, then Russia, Korea, Burma, and Vietnam. He next discusses the rebellions of the Miao and Jinchuan peoples and the uprisings on Taiwan, followed by an extensive discussion of the White Lotus rebellion. The last four chapters discuss military supplies and other issues. The text sweeps around the borders of the empire to incorporate all of the Qing's major military campaigns.

Wei Yuan's writings linked military conquest, foreign relations, and internal reform within a comprehensive historical vision. Wei put the capstone on the succession of imperial efforts to construct a fixed interpretation of the wars of expansion. His version of the Qing expansion has served as the almost unquestioned basis for subsequent accounts, and even his errors have been perpetuated by later writers. Xiao Yishan's *Qingdai Tongshi* (Comprehensive history of the Qing dynasty) of 1923, for example, incorporates verbatim, without citation, whole passages from the *Shengwuji*. James Millward has pointed out several tendentious claims of Wei Yuan, such as his deliberate underestimate of the number of troops occupying Xinjiang, which have been accepted by modern Chinese historians.[14]

Wei Yuan's treatment of Galdan's relations with Russia indicates how his approach meshed with modern nationalist history.[15] He puts particular stress on Galdan's false claim to have Russian support. Rumors of Russian aid made the Qing generals fearful, but the emperor was convinced of divine support. In Wei's view, the emperor's "extraordinary sacred power" (*shenling qiyi*) resolved all logistical problems by drawing water from the sand, causing grass to grow in the wasteland, and making ice melt on the river. It also induced natural omens that caused the despairing Galdan to commit suicide: "Every night alarming events occurred, everywhere

[Galdan] went he encountered strange omens. Fierce wind and pouring rains followed him. He knew that his followers had rebelled, and he had lost the favor of Heaven [*tianpan tianwang*], and that night or day he could be captured, so he took poison and killed himself."[14] Wei Yuan's invocation of natural forces and divine inspiration laid the foundation for all subsequent Chinese accounts of the conquest.

Geopolitics and Emperor Worship

The first Western chroniclers of the Qing conquests were the Jesuits at the court of Beijing. Father Gerbillon accompanied the Kangxi emperor on many of his northwestern campaigns and wrote an eyewitness account of them."[15] From the Jesuit reports, Western readers gained an intimate portrait of the vigorous Manchu rulers—their military prowess, their sponsorship of scholarly research, their interest in science, and, so the Jesuits hoped, their high potential for conversion to Christianity. Jean Baptiste du Halde's *Description géographique, historique, chronologique, politique, et physique de l'empire de la Chine et de la Tartarie chinoise . . .* (1735) encompassed the maximal extent of imperial China, paying special attention to the exploration and conquest of the northwest in the seventeenth century. Frenchmen saw especially close parallels to state formation and competition in Europe. It was Joseph-Anne-Marie de Moyriac de Mailla, in his *Histoire générale de la Chine* of 1708, who first compared the Kangxi emperor to Louis XIV. De Mailla's *Histoire* was one of the first general histories of China, covering the entire imperial period, and based on Chinese sources, or their Manchu translations. The early sections followed the *Zizhi Tongjian Gangmu* (Outline of the comprehensive mirror), the general history begun by Zhu Xi in the thirteenth century and continued in the Ming, but much of the Qing coverage derived from the *Fanglue* campaign histories. De Mailla devoted a large part of Volume 11 to the Galdan campaigns, contrasting the vigor and courage of the young emperor with the "perverse" character of his rival. De Mailla's account reflected closely the emerging Qing imperial view of its own achievements at a time of convergence between Western and European glorification of empire.

In the late eighteenth century, Western views of China shifted from admiration to contempt, just as the major site of contact shifted from Beijing to Canton and commercial relations replaced intellectual debate and technological exchange. England supplanted France as the dominant imperial power, consolidating its supremacy after the Seven Years' War of 1756–1763 and Clive's fortuitous victory at Plassy in India in 1757. The image of

China as a sick man gradually came to replace early impressions of the vigor of youth.

Although the empire now was much larger, British observers detected signs of weakness. As Lord Macartney commented after his embassy in 1793: "The empire of China is an old crazy, first rate man-of-war, which a fortunate succession of able and vigilant officers has contrived to keep afloat for these hundred and fifty years past, and to overawe their neighbors merely by her bulk and appearance, but whenever an insufficient man happens to have the command on deck, adieu to the discipline and safety of the ship. She may, perhaps, not sink outright; she may drift some time as a wreck, and will then be dashed to pieces on the shores, but she can never be rebuilt on the old bottom."[18] In nautical verbiage, Macartney repeated the Confucian principles of government: that disciplined operation of the state depended on the moral character of the ruler.

One of Macartney's concerns was the effect of a weakened China on the geopolitical balance in Eurasia. Macartney had spent three years at the Russian court before coming to China, signed a commercial treaty with the Russians, and written an account of the Russian empire on his return. In China he had a close relationship with Songyun, the Mongol official who had negotiated a new Treaty of Kiakhta with the Russians in 1792.

He foreshadowed the nineteenth-century geopolitical interest in China's fate when he speculated about Russian actions if the British were to occupy Macao or Lantao Island: "In such distractions would Russia remain inactive? Would she neglect the opportunity of recovering Albazin and reestablishing her power upon the Amur? Would the ambition of the great Catherine, that has stretched beyond Onalaska to the eastward, overlook the provinces and partitions within grasp at her door?"[19] Macartney, like Wei Yuan after him, saw that China's fates on the empire's continental and maritime frontiers were intertwined.

The end of the nineteenth century, the time of high imperialism, revived interest in the geopolitics of Eurasia. In 1904 the Scot Halford Mackinder first outlined his strategic vision emphasizing the predominance of great land powers over the "World Island" of Eurasia. Mackinder wrote fourteen years after the American Admiral A. T. Mahan had stressed the dominance of sea power in history.[20] Whereas Mahan's world geopolitics supported the British navy and rising American claims in the Pacific, Mackinder focused attention on Russia, Germany, and the continental powers. Mackinder's influence can be clearly detected in the later theoretical writings of Owen Lattimore and today in the writings of strategists like Zbigniew Brzezinski.[21] British and Russian competition in the "Great Game" drew the attention of swashbuckling adventurers, Foreign Office diplomats, military campaigns, and the novelist of empire, Rudyard Kipling.[22] At the same time, quite a few European historians examined in detail the battles for control of Central Eurasia between the rulers of China and their Mongolian rivals.

The works of John Baddeley, Henry Howorth, Gaston Cahen, and Maurice Courant viewed China as one of several competitive actors in a grand geopolitical competition.[23] The title of Courant's study *L'Asie Centrale aux 17e et 18e siècles: Empire kalmouk ou Empire mantchou?* epitomizes this approach. Central Eurasia is the focus; the name "China" does not appear. The two contenders are "Kalmuks" (Zunghars) and "Manchus," not "Chinese, Mongols, Russians, or any other current national definition. Baddeley likewise placed Russia, Mongolia, and China on an equal footing, and Cahen, though his title refers only to Russia and China, in fact includes a great deal of material on the Zunghar state's interactions with both Russia and China. Their imperial perspective spanning national borders saw the expansion of these three empires as a significant world process.

Chinese Historians and the Multicultural State

In the twentieth century, historical minds began to close, as China's nationalists tried to waken the people to respond to imperialist threats. Twentieth-century Chinese nationalists were most concerned with asserting the unity of "nationalities" (*minzu*) in the face of attacks from Japan, Russia, and the western European powers. Since they regarded the Manchus as alien, backward rulers of the Han race, they played down, or almost ignored, the unique features of Qing territorial expansion. For them, Manchu autocracy held back the powers of the united Chinese people, who would generate a strong nation from the bottom up. China's territorial scope dated from the unification of China under the Qin emperor in the third century BCE. Nationalists saw the progressive expansion of imperial control outward into Central Eurasia as a natural consequence of rising Chinese culture and power. They did not give the Manchus credit for expanding the Chinese realm; instead they blamed them for weakening China's position in the world.

Their cursory treatment of the conquests derived from the assumption that Qing expansion was simply a culmination of earlier Chinese dynastic projects, not a breakthrough that redefined the character of the Chinese state. The teleology of nationalist history implied that the Qing had merely fulfilled the mission of its predecessors to encompass all the territory that

"naturally" belonged to China. The modern Chinese state then inherited this space and made it the basis of China's imagined community. Modern textbook accounts that stress the continuity of the Qing with earlier dynasties implicitly assume that this remarkable territorial expansion made little difference.

But, as I have argued, Qing expansion was not simply a linear outgrowth of previous dynasties. It represented a sharp break with the strategic aims and military capabilities of the Ming dynasty. The different character of the ruling elite, their success in mobilizing interior China's resources, and the empire's diplomacy in Eurasia made it possible. This expansion in turn had long-lasting effects on the Qing's socioeconomic structures, administrative institutions, and self-concept. The Qing emperors and generals themselves believed that they had achieved something unprecedented, but they linked their achievements to those of earlier dynasties with a successful project of rewriting the history of the conquest. In the interests of creating continuity, they masked the radical implications of their achievements. Nationalists built on the legacy left by Qing official historians to create the version of China's history that predominates today.

In the medium term, the end of the Qing conquests created some of the elements that led to the collapse of the empire in the nineteenth to early twentieth century. From a longer perspective, these conquests, by fundamentally redefining China's territorial and cultural identity, laid the foundation on which the modern nation-state rebuilt itself. We have seen how the rulers developed their self-conception as universal monarchs, embracing multiple peoples with distinct but overlapping cultural traditions in the course of the expansion. There was no single sharp turning point in cultural definition, but rather an evolving consciousness of a Heaven-endowed mission to incorporate many, but not all, of the cultures of Eurasia under a single gaze.

Defining borders and eliminating rivals also meant limiting imperial claims to legitimation. Despite the emperor's boast to encompass "all under Heaven," frontier writers like Qishiyi knew better. Wei Yuan drew on his knowledge of the many rivals to Qing power across the continent. By using foreign consultants to map the extent of the empire's territory, the Qing rulers had also implicitly recognized that they occupied only one part of the earth's surface, a global space measured with universal coordinates of longitude and latitude. From Kangxi's mappings to Wei Yuan's invocation of frontier warfare, the theme of imperial expansion developed continuously as a founding element in the construction of a new national consciousness.

Here I trace briefly the historiography of the conquests in three of the nation-states that now partition the steppe.

Modern Chinese scholars have produced abundant writings on China's northwestern regions. Considering that Tibet, Mongolia, and Xinjiang together account for only 3.6 percent of the PRC's population today, scholarly print per capita must be higher here than for any other region of China. A recent index lists 8,031 articles on the subject published from 1900 to 1988, and another lists over 7,500 books and articles on the Qing dynasty alone." Needless to say, I have only skimmed the surface of this vast literature.

Regardless of the political regime, this historical writing demonstrates remarkable continuity. Ever since 1763, when the Qianlong emperor wrote his "Record of the Entire Zunghar Tribe," Qing, Republican, Taiwanese, and PRC scholars have taken very similar approaches. Han-centered nationalism overrides other methodologies, whether of the *kaozheng*, nationalist, or Marxist-Leninist school. The common narrative thread of predestined "unity" links works produced under very different political circumstances. Why is there such uncanny agreement on this basic theme?

"History" in most languages has a dual meaning: the actual lived experience of people in the past and the remembered (written or oral) record of the past. The two meanings are cyclically intertwined. Our lived experience, decisions, intentions, and ideals in the present moment derive from how we interpret our past experience. Likewise, present experience shapes historical interpretation, either as scholarly monograph or as personal memory. In reciprocating motion, present and past influence each other as our pasts and our presents cyclically evolve. Neither totally determines the other, but neither stands alone. The words used in historical production, like all words, are empty vessels, signifiers constantly being refilled with new meanings but never entirely losing the old ones." In interpreting the Qing conquest, historians have continued a cyclical ritual process, perpetuating long-standing myths while renewing them under changed conditions. I discussed earlier how mythmaking began as soon as the conquest was over. Now we begin the hermeneutic circle from its endpoint, looking back from our century to the origins of this perspective. The grand cycle of interpretation is unending; no one has the final word. Whether new perspectives are an improvement over older ones is for the reader to decide.

Russian, Chinese, and modern Mongolian scholars drastically disagree about the meaning of the defeat of the Zunghars. Chinese writers see Qianlong's victory as a natural process of incorporation of "our Mongols" into a Chinese state, and they regard Xinjiang as having always been Chinese territory. They view the Zunghars as mere rebels, deny the existence of

widespread anti-Qing sentiments among the Mongols, and ignore the fact that Xinjiang was never permanently controlled by a Chinese dynasty until the Qing. Russian writers call the Qing an aggressive, expanding empire, and they look for signs of class struggle in Mongolian national resistance against the feudal Qing state. One could say that the Russian scholars seem to be more Marxist and the Chinese more nationalist, but Russian writers justify the expansion of their empire, too, without trying to claim that Siberia "always belonged" to Russia. Contemporary Mongolian scholars assert the essential unity of the Mongolian people from earliest times, playing down their real divisiveness.

These nationalist perspectives projected back from modern times contaminate our understanding, for this was not a truly "nationalist" struggle on any side. It was a state-building struggle in which the military and political power of the rulers counted for much more than the nationalities of the people involved. All sides made appeals for mass support at times and invoked symbols of ethnic unity, including Chinggis Khan and Chinese emperors, but the outcome was decided by armies, diplomacy, and economic pressure, not by the modern weapons of newspapers, broadcasting, and mass mobilization.

"Mongol," "Manchu," "Chinese," "Uighur," and "Hui" nationalities in the modern sense did not consistently join the same side of the struggle or express uniform views. They acted to preserve their interests as towns, tribes, families, and individuals during a contest for power among coalitions of elites from disparate backgrounds. To appreciate the true complexity of the Qing's expansive drive is to gain insight into how the multiethnic empire of the Qing differed from the modern Chinese nationalist state.

Wei Yuan, as I have noted, put in place the standard account followed by historians in China ever since." But there are some interesting discrepancies worth comment. From the viewpoint of PRC historians, he committed two grave "errors." They criticize his "class biases" for favoring the repression of popular rebellion, but they find his questioning of the permanence of China's boundaries to be even more serious. He wrote that much of the territory of China defined by the Nerchinsk treaty was "wasteland" newly entered on the registers, and he noted that Taiwan "from ancient times was not part of China." The editors of the 1984 Beijing edition of the *Shengwuji* insist that "these are undoubtedly completely mistaken assertions, which do not accord with historical truth."

Wei Yuan was, of course, correct, but the idea that Qing expansion incorporated new territories violates nationalist myth. Nationalists must claim the Qing boundaries as eternally fixed, endowed by Heaven or by the course of history with natural legitimacy. The Qianlong emperor would smile to realize how successfully he had instilled this myth in the modern Chinese mind.

Dai Yi's *Concise History of the Qing Dynasty* is representative of historical work in the People's Republic of China through the 1980s." The tone of his treatment of the Central Eurasian conquests is indicated in his chapter titles: "Unification of the Minority Peoples of the Border Region and the Strengthening and Development of a Multinational Empire"; "Qing Suppression of the Zunghar Galdan's Divisive Influence and the Unification of the Northwest Region"; "Russian Aggression against Our Northern and Western Borders and Galdan's Mobilizing of the Nationalities in a Divisive [*fenlie*: splitist] Rebellion"; "Tsarist Russia's Aggression against the Zunghar Region and the Zunghar Army and People's Anti-Russian Struggles." His account focuses entirely on the creation of unity, not on the expansion of territory.

Use of the term "unification" (*tongyi*), never "conquest" (*zhengqu*), is de rigueur among Chinese historians. We may also note Dai's highly anti-Russian emphasis. In Dai's interpretation, the Zunghar people loved their territory and resisted Russian aggression against it. They rejected Russian efforts to entice them to submit to the Tsar; Dai interprets this as resistance by "our country's Mongols" against Russian aggression. Both Galdan and his enemies, the Khalkhas, resisted Russian attack in the 1670s, but Dai Yi's real hero is the Jebzongdanba Khutukhtu, who induced the Khalkhas to submit to the Kangxi emperor. Dai initially praises Galdan for resisting the Russian invasion, but after Galdan turned against the Qing, Dai stresses the support given by the Russians to Galdan (even though there is little evidence of this). The implicit territory defended by "our country's Mongols" is the maximal extent of Qing power attained only after the 1760s conquests. Dai writes his story as an inevitable progression leading finally toward the borders of the mid-eighteenth century.

Modern Chinese scholarship also makes moral judgments of personalities, reminiscent of the "praise and blame" historiography of the classical period. Ma Ruheng's article on "the [reactionary] life of Amursana" tells the story of the last Mongol prince to challenge Qing rule over the steppe. In Ma's view, Amursana had "totally negative historical significance" because he split the unity of the minority peoples. Chinese historians, says Ma, need to refute Russian and Mongolian historians who praise Amursana for resisting Qing aggression. Ma presumes that nearly all the Zunghars wanted to gain peace by submitting to the Qing. Only Amursana's "wild ambition" (*yexin*) for personal power led him to revolt." As we know, the full story is much more complex. Amursana first called in Qing aid to help him seize power against his rivals, and later rebelled when the

Qing rulers deliberately undercut his efforts to unify the Mongols. The Qing emperor insisted on a military campaign against Amursana, rejecting his cautious advisers' counsel. Qing levies on the Mongol allies for this campaign touched off a rebellion among the Eastern Mongols. Even though Qing troops quickly defeated Amursana, the military struggle itself cannot be reduced simply to his lust for power.

Ma, like Dai, also pursues the anti-Russian theme. In the view of both, Russian aims were unequivocally expansionist, with the purpose of using Amursana to control Zungharia. This interpretation is an obvious allusion to contemporary Sino-Russian conflicts. Ma correctly notes that Siberian governors observed the Zunghar Mongols closely in the 1750s, but he credits the Russians with far too much active agency. They mainly watched and waited, and did not intervene directly in Zungharian affairs.

Ma concludes that "Amursana's revolt was not a military uprising but an effort to split the nationalities backed by the Russians" (*minzu fenlie panluan*), and quotes Mao Zedong's canonical statement, "Our country is a large and populous nation composed of many different nationalities." He continues:

The Qing dynasty was a period when our unified nation of many nationalities became increasingly consolidated and developed. Qianlong's suppression of Amursana's revolt continued the tasks of Kangxi and Yongzheng of protecting the unity of the nation and waged a righteous war to resist Russian aggression. This battle not only strengthened and developed the unity of the multinational state but also coincided with the demands for unity of each of the nationalities and their common wish to oppose splitism. Therefore the victory in the war against rebellion was inevitable.[30]

This interpretation exhibits clearly the main traits of nationalist historiography: its belief in a progressive evolution toward unity, its moralistic judgment of historical actors by the standard of popular unity, and its unquestioned assumption that the multiple nationalities composing the modern Chinese nation have always shown undivided loyalty to imperial regimes.

Soviet and Mongolian Attacks on Qing Aggression

Soviet historiography and Mongolian historiography share many of these assumptions, but their evaluation of the Qing is diametrically opposed. I. Ia. Zlatkin's *History of the Zunghar Khanate, 1635–1758* is the most detailed analytical study available in a Western language. Even though he does not read Chinese, he provides very useful references to Russian archival sources.[11] He rejects Chinese and earlier European interpretations of the Zunghars as aggressive conquerors of other Mongols. Instead, he tries to demonstrate the fundamental unity of Western and Eastern Mongols with the Tibetan Buddhist church against the expansionist Manchu state. He points out that the Kangxi emperor confirmed Galdan's title of Boshoku Khan in 1679, putting them for a while on good terms. But the Qing's main goal was to prevent the formation of a unified steppe power combining the Western and Eastern Mongols. Galdan's attack on the Tüsiyetü Khan of eastern Mongolia led Kangxi to vow destruction of the Zunghars because, in essence, Galdan was trying to create an independent Mongolian nation, and the Chinese were determined to destroy it. Zlatkin, like the Chinese, believes in the natural "unity of peoples" as an underlying force in history, but he draws the boundaries differently. For him, the united Mongols unsuccessfully asserted their desire for autonomy against the coercive force of the Manchu state.[12]

Mongolian historians in independent Mongolia put the case even more strongly. For Mongolian and Soviet historians, the idea of China as a unified multinational state including the Mongolians constitutes the "Maoist falsification of history," which continues the Sinocentrism of the imperial period that began two thousand years ago.[13] They trace this Sinocentrism back to the Mandate of Heaven idea of the Zhou, which puts China at the center of civilization and regards the non-Han peoples of the northern frontier as no better than beasts. At the same time, Chinese historians argue that the northern nomadic people were always part of the Chinese cultural and national realm, so China's wars against them were internal suppressions of rebellions, not wars against an external enemy. By contrast, Mongolian historians insist that the Chinese and Mongols always were completely distinct political, geographical, and cultural units of equal status, demarcated by the Great Wall. Ironically, modern Chinese nationalist historiography, because it inherits the Qing definition of boundaries, has to play down the cultural significance of the Great Wall demarcation, while Mongolian historians overstress its importance in order to protect their autonomy.

For Mongolians and Soviets, the Chinese have been consistently expansionist, using a variety of strategies to penetrate and subjugate the nomads. They view the uprisings of Amursana and Chingünjav as national liberation movements, not "bandits' revolts." These were "popular movements" that allegedly involved all the classes and strata of Mongolian society. Vacillating feudal princes joined the Qing, but impoverished herdsmen fought

most consistently. Here we have the classic combination of Marxist-Leninist class analysis with nationalist history, in which the feudal classes become unreliable representatives of the nation while the "masses" become its most passionate defenders. We can recognize parallel arguments in Chinese historians' discussions of nineteenth-century China's relations with the West, with the decadent Manchu ruling elite subverted for the Mongolian nobility.

By contrast, C. R. Bawden points out that the loss of independence was not seen in earlier times as such a tragedy as it is today:

For the Mongols, the Manchu conquest was to mean, in modern terms, the extinction of their independence, but it is reasonable to ask what sort of independence this was, and whether, in the conditions of the seventeenth century, the loss was a true one. It is only in relatively recent years that national independence for all has come to be considered the political *summum bonum*, and it may well be that we, together with present-day Mongol historians, are . . . applying modern values to a situation to which they are not wholly applicable, by looking on the loss of independence as an evil in itself.

He argues that in the seventeenth century, there was no "cohesive sense of Mongol nationality . . . Loyalties were limited and personal," and the Mongols "had no sense of community."[14] Bawden's view is too extreme, in my opinion, but he indicates how modern interpretations exaggerate the extent of common national feeling among the Mongols before the twentieth century.

Empires, Nations, and Peoples

Clearly the Sino-Soviet split of the 1960s has affected these divergent evaluations of Qing history, but the differences go much deeper. Even in the 1980s, as the reform period began and ideological control loosened up, historians repeated the same themes. The basic assumptions about historical change on both sides are strikingly non-materialist for supposed Marxist-Leninists. They display more a search for a *volkisch* "spirit of a people" than careful attention to basic material factors. Although all three schools invoke class struggle and claim a division between nationalist "masses" and decadent "elites," they provide very little evidence of a real evolution of class consciousness based on changing modes of production. The effort to define stages of development is far less prominent in histories of this topic than the defense of the unity of peoples against foreign aggression. Until the 1980s, the three communist states whose borders met here devoted most of their historiography of the region to defining their national territory against one another. Boundary maintenance won over proletarian solidarity.

We may summarize the characteristic features of this type of historiography with four terms: *teleology, moral evaluation, natural frontiers,* and *essentialized identities.*

1. Teleology reads back causation of events in the past from present outcomes. It is not merely "present-mindedness": all historians are influenced by the concerns of their day. This particular form of present-mindedness takes the current outcome as determined and traces how past processes led up to it. It presupposes an underlying historical process independent of human action that culminates in the nation-state. It is, in effect, a Hegelian assumption about historical change, of which Marxism is only one variant. Its primary flaws are anachronism and excessive determinism. Anachronism means, for example, attributing "class consciousness" to peoples in a society without a capitalist, or even feudal, mode of production. Determinism means the assumption that those who resisted state expansion inevitably had to suffer defeat, which is to ignore the multiple contingent events that shaped the result.

2. We may also note a very strong concern with moral evaluation. Those defined as "rebels" are morally vicious, and historians like to highlight their personal weaknesses. The Chinese historians do not give the Zunghars credit for a positive ideology or a coherent program. There is a noticeable contrast between former Chinese historical treatment of Han peasant rebels, like the Taiping, who used to be seen as anticipating mass peasant revolution, and the treatment of non-Han rebels as "splitists" who endangered the unity of Han and minority peoples.

3. Territorial boundaries are assumed to be natural and predetermined, and very close to contemporary state borders. For the Chinese, "aggression" (by Russians) means the violation of these virtual boundaries even before they have been negotiated. For the Russians and Mongolians, Qing "aggression" means expansion beyond the current borders of the PRC. All national historians have invoked the idea of "natural frontiers" to justify their state's territorial control. Lucien Febvre argued strongly against this concept, showing how all state borders were constructions of a particular period.[15] Nevertheless, some states could make more plausible claims than others, since many of their "natural" boundaries followed clear geographical defining points such as mountains, rivers, and oceans. These claims become much more dubious in Central Asia, where there are no such obvious delimiting factors.

4. Likewise, ethnic identities are naturalized, essentialized, and seen as fixed. Nationalist historians try to establish a continuous genealogy by tracing names, under the assumption that "Oirats" in the Yuan, for example, are the same people as the "Weilate" in the Ming and the "Elute" in the Qing. But many of these ethnonyms referred to confederations of many different peoples, not to a single, fixed entity.

Each of these four features contains a kernel of truth. All historians are present-minded in some sense; moral evaluation is an essential component of historical interpretation; state boundaries did matter in the eighteenth century; and there was some sense of ethnic identity among the Mongols. But using these assumptions uncritically to describe inevitable outcomes of a universal historical process instead of contingent human creations gives us a highly misleading view.

By contrast, first, we need to reintroduce contingency and avoid anachronism. Empathetic identification tries to see events from the viewpoint of the actors themselves, who were not certain of the outcome. Even their goals were not fixed in advance but evolved within a fluid situation. We should be skeptical of the assumption of an underlying impersonal historical process uninfluenced by individual action.

Second, we should take a more objective stance, giving equal weight to all the players, without preconceived judgments. We must try to reconstruct the interests and motivations of the states and actors in their own terms and not interpret them as stages on the way to national states.

Third, we should see boundary consciousness as evolving and constructed, not naturally fixed. The idea of state boundaries was an emerging consciousness in eighteenth-century China, and the narratives of these territorial definitions built the framework for later nationalist historiography, but the boundaries of the Qing empire were not "there" waiting to be discovered. We should not neglect the arbitrariness in the political and social construction of boundaries of the state.

Fourth, ethnic and tribal definitions were likewise historical products of contingent interactions. They were not "primordial." As in modern discussions of the creation of ethnicity or the "invention of tradition," they came from strategies of groups looking for the most beneficial ways to define themselves in a shifting cultural context.

Finally, material factors need close attention. Access to food, water, animals, weaponry, and commercial goods was critical to the survival of these states. All three of them competed to increase their "stateness" in similar ways. They faced constraints of the natural environment, which affected productive use of resources, and of the social and political environment, which affected the willingness of primary producers to yield resources to state builders.

Today, peoples, nations, and civilizations define themselves consistently only in terms of what they are not. Lacking confidence in the stability of our own personal, social, and national identities, we look for, or invent, peoples conceived as radically different from ourselves. If we do not know securely what we have in common, surely we can agree that we have little in common with the barbarian, the primitive, the Oriental, the fundamentalist, the terrorist: in short, the fetishized Other. Michel Foucault pointed out how Western society since the eighteenth century has defined reason primarily by contrasting it with madness. Hayden White has discussed how, likewise, western Europeans examined what it meant to be civilized by creating the image of the Wild Man—an image first of the untamed primitive in the Middle Ages, which was transformed into the "noble savage" in the period of Romanticism. Even in modern social theory this technique persists. Barrington Moore argues that if we cannot agree on what kinds of societies are the best, or the most likely to provide positive values of justice, freedom, and wealth, we can at least agree on the causes of cruelty, poverty, and injustice.[16]

The power of negative thinking can be a genuine effort to examine critically the unexamined assumptions of modern culture. It can be a deconstructive tool, designed to show how Western imperial culture, in particular, has created the fictional Oriental in its own image, for its own imperial interests.[17] But seldom has this form of analysis been applied anywhere outside the modern West. If critics confine themselves to subverting Western values by showing how they depend ultimately on no fixed common core but only on a series of relative, shifting oppositions, they still implicitly find "the West" a privileged site of analysis. Why not look at Asia through the same lens?

Recent discussions of the rise of nationalism share many of the same strengths and limitations. A burgeoning literature now examines the rise of nationalist ideologies in western Europe and the Americas. Different analysts find different times and places of origin for nationalism: Benedict Anderson focuses, for example, on the role of print culture among the creole elites of nineteenth-century Latin America. Liah Greenfeld turns to sixteenth-century England. Erich S. Gruen finds "national identity" even in republican Rome. There, too, Romans sought to define their identity by contrast with the peoples they both admired and distrusted the most: the Greeks. They adopted a legend tracing the origins of Rome to Trojan, not Greek, ancestors in order to "[fit] the Romans within the matrix of Greek legend that stretched back to remote antiquity while marking a differentiation and projecting a separate identity."[18]

Once again, the use of definition by negation proves doubly produc-

tive. Nations and their peoples do in fact define themselves by opposition. Scholars of nationalism can undermine spurious claims to essential identities, claims which distort history and can lead to unthinking hostility. But only very recently has this analysis been applied to Asia, and China in particular. Dru Gladney has shown very provocatively how the definition of minorities in contemporary China as eroticized Others serves to discipline the Han majority. Edward Friedman points to the collapse of a secure "Han" identity and the growth of rival regional definitions, centered on new archaeological interpretations and the exaltation of regional cultures.[19]

The present discussion of the place of the northwest frontier in the formation of the Han identity and the role of the Qing dynasty complements these insights. The Qing completion of the northwest conquest reconfigured the identities of "China" and the "Han." The eighteenth century was not the age of nationalism in China, but it set the framework within which the late-nineteenth-century definitions of the Chinese nation had to operate. This framework included the definition of boundaries; the fixed racial and genealogical identities of Han, Manchus, Muslims, and Tibetans; and the imperial project of establishing control over multiple peoples, incorporating the non-Han peoples as subordinate Others.

Qing scholars who analyze imperial ideology should not look at the fully formed ideology of the eighteenth century in isolation. This structure of symbols, texts, inscriptions, and pronouncements defined behavior and thought for the imperial elite, its officials, and at least some of its subjects, but it evolved significantly from the seventeenth century to the eighteenth. During its construction, the Qing rulers competed with rivals who constructed their own ideologies. It was a temporary product of a particular time. By the end of the eighteenth century, the Qing rulers' tone of complacency, wholeness, and completion expressed satisfaction at the successful defeat of their enemies. Yet without barbarian enemies, they found themselves without a solution for the new challenges of the nineteenth century.

15

State Building in Europe and Asia

THE Qing conquests decisively changed the history of the Chinese empire, the Russian empire, and the Central Eurasian peoples in between. I have analyzed the Qing–Zunghar conflict as a process of competitive state building, in which both sides had to mobilize economic and military resources, build administrative organizations, and develop ideologies of conquest and rule. The Qing was not an established state facing a disorganized group of "bandits." In the early seventeenth century, the Manchus constructed a state apparatus designed for military conquest. Expansion of their state's territory remained the primary task of the dynasty's rulers until the mid-eighteenth century. At the same time, the Mongols who rejected Manchu domination also created an increasingly "statelike" apparatus of rule in Central Eurasia, one that grew from a loose tribal confederation to approach the structure of a settled regime. Both Manchus and Zunghars built a capital city, promoted agricultural settlement, sponsored trade, and developed bureaucratic procedures as part and parcel of their constant military campaigning. War fed the state as the state supplied the materials for war. The Manchus, once they had conquered the core of China, had far greater economic resources at their disposal than the Zunghars, and they inherited a transportation network that linked the crucial resources of men, grain, and money in dense systems of exchange. The Zunghars had to collect much more fragmented materials over a vast, unintegrated space, and this made their state-building project much more challenging and, ultimately, ephemeral.

Still, the Zunghars were able to hold out for a surprisingly long time against the Qing juggernaut because of two vital factors that protected them: mobility and distance. The high cost of land transport prevented the Manchus from extending their reach beyond the Great Wall unless they had Mongolian allies. Much of the Qing project through the Yongzheng reign was devoted to winning over these allies with economic lures, diplomatic alliances, and military force. Yongzheng's humiliating defeat in 1731 illustrates how the poverty and breadth of Central Eurasia imposed severe limits on the extension of Qing power.

But Yongzheng's domestic reforms laid the groundwork for future expansion by increasing bureaucratic efficiency. The Grand Council and secret palace memorials allowed Qianlong to respond quickly to economic and military needs in the far-flung northwestern domains. The establishment of civil administration in Gansu, followed by the incorporation of Qinghai, paved the way for Qianlong's later incorporation of Xinjiang. After nursing its wounds, the empire was prepared to strike back in the mid-eighteenth century. Despite a severe drought all over the northwest, officials mobilized grain, horses, soldiers, civilians, nomads, grass, uniforms, and weaponry to crush their determined foe once and for all. The steady construction of this logistical network in the midst of battle and diplomacy laid the basis for the unprecedented Qing expansion.

For their part, the Zunghars desperately tried to gather every possible resource to defend their state. They could draw on the Ili valley's fields and the oases of Turkestan. They extracted tribute from Siberian tribes until the Russians drove them out. Central Eurasian trade was a key component of the Zunghar state, as it had been for every nomadic empire. The "Bukharan" caravan traders connected the Zunghars to Russian territories and the great cities of the south. Tibet and Kokonor provided both grain and pastureland and the legitimating ideology of the Tibetan Buddhist church. Other resources lay widely scattered, from the valleys of the Irtysh, Orkhon, and other rivers to the salt and potential golden sands of lakes Yamysh and Balkash. Drawing all of these together would have taxed the greatest of rulers, even if he had not faced the ominous threat of the two huge settled empires closing in on either side.

As luck would have it, both sides did for a time have highly competent, dynamic, aggressive leadership. The Kangxi, Yongzheng, and Qianlong emperors, each in his own way, coordinated effectively the multiple organizations necessary to carry out the conquest. But they met their match in Galdan, Tsewang Rabdan, and Galdan Tseren, who devised daring responses to Qing pressure. Leadership alone did not determine the outcome, but neither was the Zunghar defeat an inevitable result of structural imbalances. The deeds of the Chinese emperors have been well recognized. At the risk of offending Chinese nationalists, I have stressed the foresight and determination of the Zunghar leaders so that their lesser-known story can be told.

The Political Ecology of Frontier Conquest

This account allows us to look at the expansion of the Qing empire on all its frontiers and to compare Qing activities with those of the other states of Eurasia. This model of political ecology brings together four crucial features of Qing military expansion: frontier relations with nomadic state builders, military strategy, logistics, and negotiations with neighboring empires.[1] In each of these areas the Qing followed precedents but went well beyond them.

The term "frontier" has two opposing meanings: it can designate either a broad zone of multiple cultural interactions or a linear border dividing two states. The first usage is predominantly American, the second mainly western European (as in the French *frontière*). The modern Chinese term *bian-jiang* combines both connotations. *Bian* signifies the periphery or borderland zone, while *jiang* (a character made up of a measuring bow and fields with berms separating them) clearly implies territorial separation. Both ideas are embedded in China's history. The Qing project was to eliminate the ambiguous frontier zone and replace it with a clearly defined border through military control, commercial integration, and diplomatic negotiations with border states.

Frontier Relations. Owen Lattimore noted that steppe nomadic empires "follow like a shadow" Chinese centralized regimes, and Thomas Barfield has elaborated upon his thesis.[2] The plausibility of this thesis rests on ecological foundations. The conditions of life in the steppe favor fragmentation. Nomads live off their livestock and move seasonally between pasturelands. If there is enough grazing land, a would-be steppe leader cannot easily establish domination over other tribal leaders because they can simply move away. So tribal rivalries and fragmentation are common. But occasionally great united steppe empires form. Why is this possible? Great empires require both personal charisma and a material basis. The resources for these empires came from outside the steppe, and primarily from China, the richest neighboring settled civilization.

As Chinese dynasties rose and fell, steppe empires rose and fell with them. Contrary to the common Chinese view, it was almost never the ambition of a steppe leader to conquer China itself. Steppe leaders staged raids on the Chinese frontier to plunder it for their own purposes. It took a long

time for the Chinese to work out an effective response. Large military campaigns gained brief successes but failed in the long run. The "tribute system" worked as an institutionalized protection racket, in which Chinese traded rich silks, porcelain, jewelry, and money for bad horses, at a loss, in return for nomads' promises to stop raids.

This regular process broke down when a steppe leader lost control of his subordinate Khans, or when a Chinese dynasty at the end of its cycle was too weak to keep up tribute payments. The collapse of a Chinese dynasty threatened the stability of the steppe empire. This relationship explains why, for example, the Uighurs intervened to keep the Tang dynasty alive after the An Lushan rebellion of 755 CE. The Yuan dynasty, which did conquer all of China, is in this perspective the major exception to this pattern, not the rule.

Under the "Manchurian alternative," like the Khitan Liao (907-1124 CE) and Jurchen Jin (1115-1234 CE) dynasties, semi-nomadic leaders conquered part of China and part of the steppe. They set up a kind of dual rule, with one form of administration and army for China and another for their nomad followers. Barfield extends the Manchurian model to cover the Qing dynasty as well.

How closely does Barfield's model of frontier relationships apply ro the Qing-Zunghar relationship? The Qing was a "Manchurian" dynasty in origin, and its rulers did establish a dual administrative system, especially in the military realm. They used both the banner system and the Han Green Standard troops for domestic control and frontier expansion. But the Qing rulers did not confine themselves to the North China plain, as the Liao and Jin did, and they did not face any rivals in the Mongolian steppe after the mid-eighteenth century. Like the anomalous Yuan, in Barfield's schema, the Qing rulers expanded far beyond the limits of the steppe-frontier interaction model. Parallels with earlier dynasties are only partial.

Commercial relations on the frontier also display only partial parallels to earlier experiences. We may note especially the continued efforts by the Zunghars to use the tribute system to increase the resources of their state. They requested that more embassies be allowed to go to Beijing, each with as many as two thousand men. Once Qing officials perceived the Zunghars as a threat, they severely restricted the number of tribute embassies. On the one hand, these embassies brought revenue for the Zunghars, as they did for earlier nomadic state builders. On the other hand, the Qing did not have to buy off the nomadic raiders because of their military weakness. Except for a short period in the early eighteenth century, the Qing court kept military pressure on its rivals. Trade was a useful complement to military expansion, not an inadequate substitute for it.

Omeljan Pritsak gives more weight than Barfield to the autonomous activity of traders in forming new states in the steppe. He has argued that an "international trading class" interacting with the nomadic Khazar confederation created the state of Rus' in the tenth century. Barfield, however, tends to examine only relations between nomadic state builders and Chinese officials and merchants, whereas many caravan traders were beyond Chinese state control. In our case, the Zunghars made substantial efforts to draw on commercial resources beyond the Chinese tribute system. They established contacts with "Bukharan" caravan traders, and they aimed to negotiate profitable terms of trade with Russians in Siberia. Our model of frontier state formation needs to incorporate at least four separate actors: nomadic state builders, caravan traders, and both the Chinese and Russian states, instead of only two.

Military Strategy. The classic nomad military response to an approaching Chinese army was the same as Mao Zedong's: withdrawal in the face of superior numbers. Unlike Chinese armies, which depended on supplies from agricultural settlements, the nomads could simply move away until the Chinese had stretched their supply lines too far, then turn around and ambush them. This practice led to numerous Chinese defeats. Han Wudi's long expedition to Central Asia to obtain the "blood-sweating" horses of Ferghana is the classic example. He did get his horses, but only 20 percent of the troops returned. The main cause of losses to the army was inadequate supplies, not combat casualties.[3]

To annihilate nomadic armies, Qing generals had to block their escape routes. They sent three separate armies against Galdan in a pincer attack, hoping to trap Galdan's troops from the rear while the main force attacked in front. This strategy, originated by the Mongols under Chinggis Khan, required difficult feats of coordination of large masses of troops across great distances.[4] It succeeded, but just barely.

Logistics. Massive logistical preparation was the key to such mobilization. The inability of the Chinese to supply large armies in the field for long periods of time created a fundamental barrier to major steppe expeditions. From the Han dynasty up through the end of the seventeenth century, no major military force launched from the core of China could spend much more than ninety days in the steppe. Kangxi's first expedition against Galdan lasted roughly sixty days, his second one ninety-nine days, and his third ninety-one days. In each case he had to turn back because of supply limitations. Until they overcame this logistical barrier, Chinese rulers could never permanently eliminate nomadic autonomy by military means. The Qing only crossed this threshold in the mid-eighteenth century by building a chain of military magazines and supply lines into the steppe.

The resources for these supply routes had to come either from subordinated nomads or from the Chinese peasantry of the northwest, but both of these poor groups could provide only limited amounts. By the mid-eighteenth century, increasing demands for horses, sheep, and human labor touched off the Chingunjav revolt. Military demands on northwestern peasants further increased their suffering from famine and drought. Only the commercialization of the eighteenth-century economy as a whole allowed Qing officials to purchase large supplies on the markets of northwest China and ship them out to Xinjiang. Even though the price of grain in Gansu tripled, the empire-wide civilian granary system, another crucial innovation of the mid-Qing, was able to relieve enough famine-stricken peasants to prevent revolt.

Diplomacy. All Qing efforts would have been in vain if the Zunghars had had unlimited space in which to retreat. Instead, the Sino-Russian treaties constrained their mobility. Both empires agreed to set boundaries and to return refugees who crossed their borders, hindering the Zunghars from recruiting migrants, refugees, or deserters and preventing them from withdrawing out of the reach of Qing troops. Thus the Nerchinsk and Kiakhta treaties, often viewed only as an episode in Sino-Russian relations, made possible the closure of the steppe. The presence of the Russian empire in Siberia rendered Qing—steppe relations radically different from those in any earlier period.

In summary, this model of Qing expansion unites frontier relations, military strategy, logistics, and diplomacy to explain why only in the eighteenth century could a dynasty ruled from Beijing eliminate its nomadic rivals and create the largest empire in Chinese history. Unlike nationalist histories, which view the Qing as the inexorable culmination of earlier imperial projects, this perspective stresses the unpredictability of frontier conquest. Qing emperors, generals, and officials knew well that they were venturing into uncharted terrain, militarily and politically. Only later did they reinterpret all the events as predestined. Before placing the Qing conquests within Chinese and world-historical contexts, we need to recapture the uncertainty that faced the proponents of this unprecedented Great Enterprise.

I turn next to a critique of two comparative historical traditions: political theories that rely primarily on the western European experience, and theories of nomadic state formation. Usually these theories do not address each other's concerns at all. The first focus on the experience of Europe since 1500 and, later, the rest of the modern world; the second address primarily the Middle East and Central Eurasia in the premodern era. The Qing-Zunghar conflict, however, includes elements of both. Here I give only a schematic summary of some of the theoretical perspectives and suggest what can be done with them.

European, Chinese, and Inner Asian Models

Perhaps the most common approach in the first tradition is to deny the relevance of state building at all to most of Asia before the European impact in the nineteenth century. Asian state building, like nation formation, is seen as a derivative phenomenon, driven primarily by the "response to the West." Theorists tend to consider China, India, and the Ottomans as "agrarian empires," under a separate category from European "states." Yet the reasons for distinguishing "empires" from "states" seem unconvincing.

To be sure, obvious differences in scale appear to support this distinction. The *Qing* at its maximal extent controlled a land area of over 11 million square kilometers, larger than all of Europe to the Urals, and its population of about 300 million in 1800 was approximately the same as Europe's. No European state (except Russia) approached even one-tenth of this size. But this distinction looks only at the end result, not the formation of the Qing state. During its century and a half of creation, from circa 1616 to 1760, the scope of imperial control grew from a few thousand tribal people to a huge empire of hundreds of millions. In the sixteenth to *eighteenth* centuries, European states also expanded rapidly, either on the continent, as with Sweden, Prussia, and Muscovy, or overseas, like Portugal, Spain, the Netherlands, England, and France. If we take expansion itself as the common element and not simply size at the end, we can find elements of comparison. Rulers seeking to increase their span of control faced similar problems: how to win allies, how to mobilize resources, how to defend against rivals. Less important than ultimate size was the relative rate and direction of expansion. England and France developed more slowly on land than Prussia and Muscovy, but they still shared features with them.

Another political approach, strongly influenced by later nationalist historiography, assumes that western European states incorporated more "homogeneous" populations than either eastern Europeans or the non-Western world. But more recently, many historians have come to realize that national homogeneity in France or England was made, not born.[5] Multiple religious, economic, and social traditions survived within the modern nation. The recent reassertion by regions within European nation-states of their distinctive characteristics reveals the ineradicable multiplicity of state and nation building.[6] In this respect, too, European state and nation building comes to resemble more closely that of empires. We cannot so firmly divide

apparently ramshackle empires from streamlined early modern states. European states had more patchwork under the surface, and empires had more homogeneity, than we once thought.

Eric Hobsbawm and David Landes make the opposite argument: that Europe was more diverse than Asia. For Landes, the fragmentation of European states allowed for greater intellectual, commercial, and technological creativity because entrepreneurial and dissident groups could escape oppression by fleeing to a rival prince.[7] Hobsbawm claims that nationalist ideologies originated in nineteenth-century Europe as a homogenizing project, driven by the need to bring together people in political communities unified by common languages and historical traditions. The great conflicts of Europe were a product of its diversity, which created unsolvable tensions when peoples of different languages, religions, and cultures lived as neighbors on the same soil. By contrast, "China, Korea and Japan . . . are indeed among the extremely rare examples of historic states composed of a population that is ethnically almost or entirely homogeneous." These Asian states, in his view, had much less difficulty adopting nationalism because they were already more homogeneous than Europe, and had inherited longstanding bureaucratic state structures.[8] Here the Marxist historian and the worshipper of capitalism both betray their Eurocentric biases. Clearly, we can find just as much diversity within Asian societies as in Europe, and there *was no easy transition from premodern to modern nation-states* in any East Asian country: Japan, Korea, and Han China each contained many conflicting social and cultural elements. The northwest frontier of China displayed these conflicts in the sharpest, most violent fashion, making it a useful diagnostic for related tensions elsewhere. By this measure, too, Asian empires and kingdoms are not radically distinct from Europe.

Immanuel Wallerstein also sharply divides empires and the "world system" of interacting European states.[9] Wallerstein argues that during the eighteenth century, the expanding European world system drew into its orbit four regions that had previously been unconnected "external arenas": Russia, the Ottoman empire, India, and West Africa.[10] This incorporation of the periphery in the eighteenth century, Wallerstein argues, later characterized the European impact on China in the nineteenth century.

Hobsbawm, Wallerstein, and Landes all find in the fragmentation of Europe the source of the dynamism that led it to conquer the world. Unlike nationalists, they stress the interaction of the state units in Europe *with one another* rather than the distinctive characteristics of a single state. But they limit this dynamic only to Europe. Everywhere else is outside the world system, or subsumed under the term "ancient empires."

Many have disputed these claims for the distinctiveness of the European state system. Other world system theorists, like Janet Abu-Lughod and Andre Gunder Frank, argue that there has long been only one global economy encompassing a large portion of the Eurasian continent, not a unique European structure that expanded to the rest of the world.[11] They find Wallerstein's distinction between "external arenas" and "peripheries" to be artificial. Abu-Lughod and Frank differ on the timing of the emergence of a pan-Eurasian world system—Abu-Lughod finds it emerging in the thirteenth century after the Mongol conquests, while Frank claims that it existed even in prehistoric times—but they agree that Europe had no special economic features. It was a late and sudden new participant in a well-established exchange network that crisscrossed land and sea routes for many centuries.

This debate focuses on how state units interact with the larger system. For Wallerstein, the only significant impacts come from foreign trade, and a state is part of the world system only when its import-export trade decisively transforms production relations and state structures within it. Before the eighteenth century, Eastern Eurasia was outside the European world system because its trade consisted mainly of "luxury" goods which did not demand a restructuring of institutions and agrarian modes of production. The "one world system" camp, by contrast, insists that "tributary trade" relations and other modes of cultural and political interaction before the European expansion did link the major civilizations and did have effects on their internal structures. Most notably, the rise and fall of empires depended on flows of goods that supported their ability to resist both domestic and foreign rivals. If military and state power are not directly derived from trade but have an independent dynamic, and if interaction between major states strongly affects their military structures, then Wallerstein's exclusion of the Eastern Eurasian empires is based on too narrow a specification of what drives historical change.

Wallerstein also does not explore the reasons why the "external" states allowed the Europeans in. He regards the weakening of the Asian states as a natural consequence of involvement in export trade, yet at the same time he admits that commercial revenues from controlled "ports of trade" could also strengthen central power. This is just what the Qing did with the customs revenues from Guangdong, which went directly into the imperial household department. If increased trade per se does not weaken central power, there must be some other factor at work.

I side with those who do not find a strong contrast between the Qing empire and the European state system until the mid-eighteenth century. As long as the Qing rulers faced serious rivals, they had to build structures to support substantial, extended military campaigns. The mobiliza-

tion needed for these campaigns had effects well beyond the military: it also transformed the fiscal system, commercial networks, communication technology, and local agrarian society. The need to ship large amounts of military supplies into Central Eurasia constantly put pressure on localities, especially in northwest and North China, but even provinces in South China were indirectly affected through the grain tribute moving up the Grand Canal. Provisioning, military and civilian, became a key concern of the Qing because it was essential to preserve the welfare of the people at the same time the state extracted a surplus from them for security needs. The early Qing empire, then, was not an isolated, stable, united "Oriental empire" but an evolving state structure engaged in mobilization for expansionist warfare.

After the mid-eighteenth century this dynamic changed. Now there were no autonomous armed rivals beyond the reach of imperial control. Every region that was a potential threat had "entered the registers" (ru bantu) of administrative and military supervision. Of course, this map was as much mythical as real. The Kazakhs, for example, were autonomous tribes beyond the Qing's reach, but they were treated as loyal "tributaries," quite different from the hostile Zunghars. Changing vocabulary was as important as changing facts on the ground. By defining who was included and who was excluded, and expunging those who had been eliminated, Qing historians worked to stabilize the realm. Our image of a complacent, patronizing regime applies closely only to the late eighteenth century. The empire did not diverge from Europe until this late date.

In sum, the models that argue for distinctive features of a European state system, marked by pluralism, competition, or special core-periphery structures, draw an oversimplified contrast between western Europe and the rest of the Eurasian world. They ignore analogous features found in Eastern Eurasia until 1750, and they fail to assess accurately the interactions between commercial exchange and military force across the continent.

Charles Tilly's model of the formation of the European state system from 990 to 1990 offers more useful comparative insights for the study of Eurasian state building. Unlike many of the world system theorists, he focuses on the twin dynamics of the accumulation of capital and the concentration of coercive force in an environment of nearly unceasing international war. Tilly distinguishes three paths that culminated in the modern national states of Europe. In the *capital-intensive* path, followed mainly by city-states like Venice and Genoa, and by the Dutch republic, "rulers relied on compacts with capitalists ... to rent or purchase military force, and thereby warred without building vast permanent state structures." In the *coercion-intensive* mode, "rulers squeezed the means of war from their own populations and others they conquered, building massive structures of extraction in the process." Brandenburg-Prussia and Muscovy-Russia illustrate this strategy best. In between lie England and France, whose capitalized-coercion mode involved some of each, where "holders of capital and coercion interacted on terms of relative equality." [12]

Tilly's mapping of state formation onto relative concentrations of coercive and capitalist power is, as he recognizes, quite similar to G. William Skinner's discussion of the distribution within the Chinese empire of administrative and commercial resources. Both Europe's state formation and China's imperial formation can be described as the interaction of "the bottom-up building of regional hierarchies based on trade and manufacturing" with "the top-down imposition of political control" or the spatial logic of capital and coercion, respectively." [13] Unlike the world system theorists, Tilly allots considerable autonomy to the state itself. Both trade flows and security demands created by the anarchic international environment shape its interests.

Tilly's account, however, neglects nuances that appear in frontier regions. He treats Russia, for example, as an entirely coercive state, expanding in a region of vast landed resources and very little concentrated capital. In his view, Russian Tsars had little in the way of wealth to offer their followers; instead, they gave out land." [14] This view unduly minimizes the role of mercantile wealth in the building of the Russian state. Under Mongol rule, Russian princes constantly traveled to the Khan's capital at Sarai on tribute missions, which also provided them with valuable connections to the riches of the Byzantine empire. Later, in the seventeenth century, Russian merchants gained valuable privileges from cooperating with the Tsar, who relied on them for essential goods." [15] Moscow delegated the exploitation of the natural resources of Siberia, in particular, to prominent merchant families like the Stroganovs. Military and bureaucratic power still dominated, but with the assistance of a substantial mercantile component—one which is especially visible on the empire's edges.

These considerations suggest how China may fit into Tilly's scheme. At one point he seems to put China "outside the system," dividing it off as an "empire" from the "national states" of Europe. Nevertheless, Tilly also recognizes the salience of warfare in Chinese empire building and the empire's dependence on commercial resources. The "main message" of his book highlights the parallel evolution of urban hierarchies and marketing systems, the construction of state apparatuses of coercion and extraction in both societies." [16]

If the processes are similar enough to be comparable, which path of development fits China best? At first glance, the coercive-intensive mode

seems to include both China and Russia. Merchants and imperial officials did not meet on an equal footing; the bureaucratic system clearly had the edge in formally recognized power. When the empire was securely unified, its scale far surpassed that of any individual merchant's wealth.

Yet beneath the orthodox mask of bureaucratic uniformity was a landmass of astonishing diversity, whose social forms and ecological conditions were just as varied as Europe's. Skinner's model illustrates how the standardized bureaucratic structure accommodated itself to the great range of concentration of commercial and agrarian resources. Different regions of China varied systematically in the relative weight of mercantile, coercive, and redistributive institutions. I have described the problems that imperial governance faced in the northwest in allocating limited resources to a region of poor harvests and military vulnerability. Broadly speaking, the northwest had the greatest concentration of coercive force, as the south and southeast coasts had the most powerful merchant classes. Redistributive resources represented by the "evernormal" granary system followed that of the military units, with the highest per capita reserves concentrated on the less commercialized peripheries." [17]

If coercion is not the whole story, in Russia or in China, Tilly's three-way division boils down into two: the rather anomalous capital-intensive mode of the Italian city-states and of the Dutch, and the mixed capital-coercive mode of the rest of Eurasia.

Even China's northwest did not totally lack commercial resources. Its trading system bridged China's interior and Central Eurasia, with routes bringing grain from the interior and taking textiles out the Gansu corridor to the Silk Road. The Qing expanded some of these linkages to an unprecedented extent and cut off others. Heavy promotion of merchant and official grain movements from North China to Shaanxi, and from Shaanxi to Gansu, built up a new level of grain flows to the poorest regions, and the promotion of currency circulation and increased copper cash supplies generated greater local market exchange. Coercion and capital supported each other here, but coercion led the way. Military units received primary consideration, but the emperor and his officials recognized that they could not allow the military to burden the people excessively.

As long as the frontier expanded, coercive and commercial representatives joined in a common cause. The end of expansion, however, allowed other tensions to surface. Each region of the empire then faced distinctive types of social conflict. R. Bin Wong has described the outbreak of grain riots in Hunan province, for example, as a consequence of the extension of market relations to new districts, much as in early modern France. These blockages of grain flows represented protests by local consumers, often backed by local officials, who aimed to protect their own production against outside demands from merchants or higher-level officials." Gansu, by contrast, so far as I can tell, never had any grain riots, despite the fact that external demands on its grain reserves were extremely high. It could be that the active mobilization of granary reserves, as seen in the famine years 1756-1760, successfully staved off resistance, or, just as plausibly, that the heavy military presence in the province provided substantial repressive force.

Gansu still had its own way of sabotaging imperial goals. We have seen two examples: the relief scandal of 1781 and the outbreak of Muslim rebellions from the 1780s to 1820. The first represented collusion between provincial officials and outside merchants against the local peasant producers and urban consumers; the second grew from feuding between different factions of Muslim and Han villagers into protests against Han immigration and Qing rule." These were distinctive forms of resistance to state authority found in frontier regions. Whereas the first represents the victory of capital over bureaucratic control, the second signifies the outbreak of local violence against central coercion. The closing of the Chinese frontier allowed these contradictory impulses to grow large toward the end of the eighteenth century.

Tilly's model, then, although it does not focus on China or on frontiers, helps to orient our discussion toward the interplay of military and commercial forces during the time of Qing expansion. Military considerations were primary, but not exclusive, in defining the empire's identity.

R. Bin Wong also finds many common features between Qing China and early modern European socioeconomic structures. But for him, the vital concern of the imperial regime with provisioning the people derives from a special ethical tradition that has Confucian roots, ever since Mencius urged rulers to act benevolently by ensuring the welfare of their people. This attitude led in practical terms to the concept of "storing wealth among the people" (cangfu yumin), including both lowering levels of taxation and developing an empire-wide structure of evernormal granaries, which sold grain to level prices and provide famine relief.[20]

Broadly speaking, I agree with Wong's description of the Qing imperial structure, but I have a different view of its underlying motivations. In his references to grain provisioning, Wong describes the Chinese imperial ideology as holding the same orientation from classical, pre-imperial times up through the nineteenth century. There certainly was substantial continuity from one dynasty to another, and the classical texts served as reference points for all subsequent discussions, but the evolution of provisioning ideology over time indicates, once again, the prominence of military considerations as much as ethical concerns.

In 81 BCE a defense crisis on the northwest frontier had initiated a discussion of state monopolies and price-leveling sales known as the Salt and Iron Debates. Each side of the argument claimed that only its policies would increase welfare and security. The hard-liners, or statecraft strategists, argued for increased revenues from state monopolies and grain sales. The "soft-liners" (ru) argued that the burdens of excessive taxation turned peasants into exhausted soldiers discontented with imperial government. The arguments were both Mencian and strategic.[21] During the policy debates begun by Wang Anshi in 1069-1076 CE, arising from the Song's inability to hold off attack from the Liao, grain provisioning arguments were also closely connected to defense needs.

In short, it is useful but too simple to draw a direct connection between the concern of Mencius for popular welfare and the construction of the vast granary provisioning system in the Qing. Furthermore, we cannot explain the long-term survival of the imperial system solely in terms of a patrimalistic interest in the welfare of its subjects. Just as important was the hardheaded realism that recognized military force as the basis of the state, for both internal repression and external war. Wong echoes others who stress China's anti-military orientations by contrast with the aggressive West. But imperial rule relied on both welfare and warfare; each needed the other. The balance between the two shifted over time, but neither disappeared. Imperial China's security concerns, again, were not radically different from those of European states.

Instead of singing out features present in Europe and absent in China, we would do better to think in terms of major and minor themes in both. Like a symphony with several musical themes, each of which over time comes to the fore, both civilian and military provisioning played a role in state policies. Sometimes they complemented each other, and sometimes one was sacrificed to the other. In the relief campaign of 1756-1760, officials struggled mightily to blend both harmoniously, using civilian supplies for military needs and military transport for civilian use.

Grain provisioning aimed both to keep the population healthy and to support the troops in the field. It took a full-court press, mobilizing the resources of nearly the entire empire, to make this policy work. In less happy times, most conspicuously in much of the nineteenth century, grain flows were constantly diverted from civilian to military use. But sometimes the balance tilted the other way, as when Yongzheng deliberately cut back troop concentrations in order to spare resources for the peasantry. Perhaps he even went too far, starving his garrison in Mongolia into defeat. Images of a pendulum swing, or symphonic harmony and disharmony, between military and civilian provisioning put Qing policies more in line with those of European states and give us a richer view of how grain policy worked.

LEGACIES AND IMPLICATIONS

Frontier perspectives enrich our understanding of how empires sustain their core populations.

<u>Guide to Reading Timothy Parsons' Chapter "British Kenya: The Short Life of the New Imperialism" from *The Rule of Empires*</u>

1. Parson's book draws connection among a number of empires and basically links them all to the same set of attributes. What are these attributes?

2. Do you recognize events from prior readings or lectures, and if so what are they?

3. What was "new" about the "new imperialism?"

4. What was old about the "new imperialism?"

5. The separate territories and distinct cultures of empires were connected; people and ideas moved around empires. What evidence is there of these movements in Kenya?

6. Empires cannot endure merely by the application of external force. They benefit from the participation of segments of the subject population. What enables this division? List example. Does the concept of agency apply in these circumstances?

7. Did the 'cooperation' end with the demise of imperial rule?
8. What evidence is there that the British fundamentally were not in control?

9. What is counter-insurgency? How and where did it clash politically with the ideals of the new imperialism?

6

BRITISH KENYA

The Short Life of the New Imperialism

In 1905, some 373 years after Atawallpa met Pizarro on the plaza of Cajamarca, the Nandi *orkoiyot* Koitalel arap Samloei encountered another imperial entrepreneur in the highlands of Kenya. This heir of the conquistadors was a commissioned British military officer named Richard Meinertzhagen. In 1905, he was on secondment to the King's African Rifles (KAR), Britain's ragtag but grandly named East African colonial army. Unlike the Inka ruler, Koitalel was fully aware that this twentieth-century imperial soldier was a serious threat. Indeed, for the previous decade the Nandi had fought a war of attrition against the encroaching British Empire.

At first glance, it might seem odd that a supposedly "tribal" people such as the Nandi held a "modern" western power at bay for over ten years when the Inkas had succumbed to Pizarro and the conquistadors so quickly. Firmly entrenched in the cool, well-watered East African highlands, the Nandi had a conventional mixed agricultural and pastoral economy. Politically, they had no centralized institutions of authority and could be properly described as stateless. In the late nineteenth century, they divided their lands into six or seven counties (*emotinwek*) of two thousand to five thousand people under councils of elders (*kokwotinwek*) at which any married man could speak. In times of crisis special councils consisting of the most influential Nandi elders, military leaders, and ritual experts (*orkoiik*) made the key decisions.

The Nandi may have been stateless, but they were a significant military power in the highlands. In the decades before the British

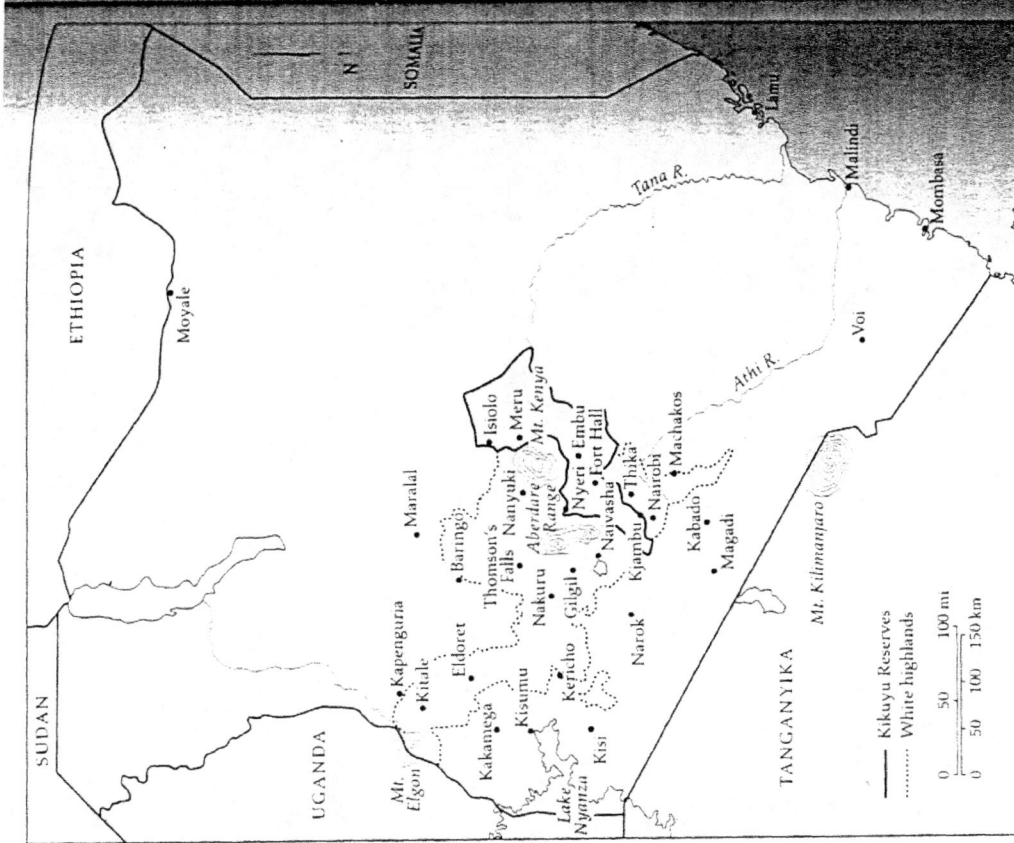

Kenya

289

arrival, victories over neighboring communities allowed them to assimilate conquered populations and acquire new crops and technologies. Known originally as the Chemwal, they earned the name Mnandi from the coastal ivory traders whose caravans they raided repeatedly. This was the Swahili word for "cormorant," a bird with a reputation for rapaciousness in East Africa.

The rising Nandi fortunes were largely the work of an influential family of orkoiik that used their ability to divine the future to usurp the authority of the kokwotinwek councils. These ritual experts were actually refugees from a nearby Maasai community who took control of important agricultural and initiation rituals after finding refuge with a Nandi clan. The orkoiyot Kimnyole arap Turukat, who was Koitalel's father, organized the Nandi regiments into a powerful military force that drove off the Maasai and raided their remaining neighbors for cattle.

Later, the British claimed that these "witch doctors" were tyrannical autocrats, but the Nandi warriors beat Kimnyole to death in 1890 after he led them on a disastrous raid that resulted in the death of five hundred of their comrades. Nevertheless, Koitalel and his brother Kipchomber arap Koilegei retained significant influence in Nandi society and waged a fierce succession struggle to assume their father's place. Koitalel enjoyed the backing of an aggressive younger faction of Nandi warriors who wanted to continue the cattle raids, which gave him the means to drive his brother into exile. With his power secure, he directed the Nandi recovery from the epidemics, cattle blight, drought, locusts, and famine that disastrously weakened the East African highland communities at the turn of the twentieth century. The Nandi were therefore much better prepared than their neighbors to face the British imperial menace.

Richard Meinertzhagen personified that threat. When he met Koitalel under the equivalent of a flag of truce he did so as the military representative of the East Africa Protectorate (EAP), which became the Colony and Protectorate of Kenya in 1920. The EAP was actually the successor state to the anemic Imperial British East Africa Company (IBEAC), a chartered company that the metropolitan British government used to stake its initial claim to the region. The European chartered company was a powerful imperial tool in the early modern era, but it was an ineffectual anachronism in the late nineteenth century. Although the IBEAC reserved a slice of East Africa

for Britain, its small and ill-equipped private army could not cope with the Nandi and other powerful local forces. Under both Kimnyole and his son Koitalel the Nandi raided passing caravans and stole copper telegraph wire and raw materials from construction parties building a railway from the port of Mombasa to Uganda. The EAP, which replaced the company in 1895, mounted successive "pacification campaigns" against them, but the Nandi wisely avoided a direct confrontation with its Maxim guns and other western firearms.

Fed up with Nandi intransigence, the British demanded that Koitalel and his followers pay a fine of three hundred cattle or face the consequences. They knew full well that the Nandi would refuse, and Meinertzhagen was part of a massive punitive expedition consisting of eighty British officers, fifteen hundred African soldiers and policemen, thirty-five hundred armed and unarmed porters, one hundred Somali "levies," one thousand Maasai "auxiliaries," ten machine guns, and two armored trains. This represented the protectorate's ultimate solution to the Nandi problem.[1] The Nandi Field Force's mission was to provoke the Nandi into standing and fighting by seizing their cattle. The Nandi elders' protests that they had little authority over Koitalel and his reckless younger followers were of no consequence.

The British framed their East African imperial project in moral and humanitarian terms. Denying that they were conquerors, they claimed that military force was the only way to compel the backward peoples of the highlands to respect civilized authority. By their count, the Nandi transgressions included the murder of Europeans, straightforward theft, and, most significant, demonstrating to other African communities that it was possible to defy imperial Britain. It mattered little that most of the Nandi's European victims were part of a marginal, often brutal rabble who sought to enrich themselves by leveraging their privileged status as "white men." They were clearly heirs of the Pizarrists, but the absence of lootable empires in the highlands forced them to seek their fortunes through cattle theft, petty fraud, and thinly disguised slave raiding. The Nandi recognized these men for what they were. Responding in kind, they murdered a British "trader" who had tortured two alleged cattle thieves to death. Even Meinertzhagen admitted that a grasping protectorate official provoked the Nandi by using punitive expeditions as an excuse to confiscate their cattle, which they kept primarily for themselves.

Yet Meinertzhagen was equally representative of the marginal men who sought wealth and status through empire in the highlands. While he disdained the company employees who were driven by simple greed, he and his fellow military officers sought fame and rapid promotion by winning glory on African battlefields. Likening the Nandi people to "a troublesome schoolboy" that had to be whipped, he had no reservations about using brutal and morally questionable tactics to achieve his goals. He admitted frankly in his memoirs: "I have no belief in the sanctity of human life or in the dignity of the human race. Human life has never been sacred; nor has man, except for a few occasional cases, been dignified."[2]

Meinertzhagen put this ruthless pragmatism into practice when he met Koitalel on October 19, 1905, to discuss a truce. The Nandi *orkoiyot* did not make Atawallpa's mistake in underestimating an invading foreigner, but he still made the fatal error of assuming that Meinertzhagen would behave honorably. Claiming that Koitalel was plotting an ambush, the British officer brazenly shot the *orkoiyot* to death when the two leaders met to shake hands. Meinertzhagen's men then opened fire and killed twenty-three more members of Koitalel's entourage. Accounts differ, but it appears that Koitalel was holding nothing more than a bundle of grass, which was the Nandi symbol for peace. In retelling the ambush story in his memoirs, Meinertzhagen professed to like the Nandi and claimed that he saved them from further destruction by removing a tyrant.[3]

Pizarro would have approved, but this tested the British liberal sympathies of the time. Although Meinertzhagen faced three separate army review boards to answer for his actions, there was no denying that the death of the *orkoiyot* broke the back of the Nandi resistance. The Nandi Field Force killed six hundred warriors and seized ten thousand of their cattle, which largely went into the herds of the rival Maasai. A follow-up punitive expedition killed fifty more people, seized more livestock, and burned almost 150 acres of crops. Faced with starvation, the Nandi capitulated. Under the terms of the peace settlement, they surrendered large sections of territory to the railway and European settlement.

Eventually, Meinertzhagen's superiors covered up the incident by recommending him for the Victoria Cross. He went on to distinguish himself in the First World War as the chief intelligence officer in Palestine and a friend of T. E. Lawrence, an aid at the Paris Peace

Conference, and the military advisor to the postwar Colonial Office. Upon retirement he achieved an additional measure of fame as an ornithologist with an enormous collection of stuffed birds ("study skins") and as a chronicler of Lawrence. It was only decades after his death that it came to light that he had stolen many of these specimens from other collections, plagiarized a book on Arabian birds, and written his supposedly contemporaneous diary entries about Lawrence in the 1950s.[4] Meinertzhagen's success and wealth never reached the levels of the conquistadors or nabobs, but he was reasonably typical of the "civilized" men who conquered Kenya for the British Empire.

The conquest of the highlands and Britain's rapid imperial expansion in the late nineteenth century were surprising given that Europeans appeared to have sworn off conventional imperial projects after the quick demise of Napoleon's continental empire. In Europe and to some extent North America, conquest and prolonged occupation now provoked violent resistance as westerners defiantly rejected imperial subjecthood as a violation of their natural rights as citizens of a nation. Many Britons accepted the loss of their North American colonies because they were confident in their global economic and strategic dominance in the postwar era. Many concluded that formal empire was an expensive tyrannical relic, particularly after the Indian Mutiny and the steady transition of the Canadian and Australian colonies to self-governing dominions by midcentury. Mindful of Adam Smith's attack on empire as a source of war, corruption, and financial drain, John Bright, Richard Cobden, and other free traders openly questioned the value of the remaining overseas territories.

These anti-imperial sentiments were at the root of Sir Charles Adderley's call to withdraw from West Africa in the 1860s. Arguing that disease made British naval bases and enclaves in the Gold Coast, Lagos, Freetown, and the Gambia "notoriously unfit for occupation by the Anglo-Saxon race," the member of Parliament charged that they were expensive luxuries that drew Britain into costly wars. Even more problematic, their inhabitants paid no taxes and thus contributed nothing to the one-million-pound annual maintenance costs of the naval bases. The proposal to withdraw from West Africa appeared radical, but only missionaries and palm oil merchants made the case for keeping a presence in West Africa. Adderley acknowledged the importance of tropical products, but in 1865 his Select Committee on Africa (Western Coast) concluded that while it was not yet possible to give up the coastal settlements, the British government should still "encourage in the natives the exercise of those qualities which may render it possible for us more and more to transfer to them the administration of all the Governments, with a view to our ultimate withdrawal from all, except, probably, Sierra Leone."[5]

These "natives" were mostly westernized Sierra Leonean Krios, who were descended from rescued slaves, black North American loyalists, and poor Britons of African descent. Adderley's committee wanted to make the West African enclaves more efficient by partnering with these Afro-Victorians to advance British interests. The Krios and other western-educated Africans warmly embraced this recommendation because they assumed that they would become the privileged imperial class in the West African territories. Their newspapers in Sierra Leone and the Gold Coast therefore openly advocated expansion into the interior, but they had no idea that in just a few short years they would be disenfranchised by the new imperialism's inherent racism.

In the 1860s, however, they had an important role in Adderley's vision of an informal empire. Arguing that Britain did not need permanent control to advance trade and investment, this pragmatic coalition of cost-cutters and free-traders assumed that the era of formal empire was over. They believed that this was true not only in sub-Saharan Africa and other remote places but also in Latin America, where British merchants and industrialists found profitable outlets for trade and investment without having to reimpose imperial rule on the former Spanish colonies. With most of continental Europe still struggling to recover from the Napoleonic wars, the British had no serious rivals at midcentury. In Africa, apart from the French conquest of Algeria and steady expansion up the Senegal River valley, British merchants largely had the continent to themselves until the 1870s.

This is not to say, however, that the British ever intended to give up their empire. In fact, the formal British Empire continued to grow by approximately one hundred thousand square miles per year during this period, but most of the new acquisitions were strategically important naval bases or bits of territory claimed by the increasingly autonomous "white" settlement colonies in Australia, Canada, and South Africa. When the British public looked with pride on the pink-hued territories on the globe, they were gazing at these territories and not

the tropical regions that became the hunting grounds of men such as Meinertzhagen.

British politicians lost faith in their network of informal influence and free trade only after European rivals, and to a lesser extent the United States and Japan, reentered the global arena as industrial and commercial powers. While British manufacturers still turned out simple products such as textiles and hardware, their continental rivals leapfrogged ahead in the production of steel, chemicals, and electrical goods. Consequently, Britain's share of global manufacturing output shrank from 33 percent to just 14 percent between 1870 and 1914. To make matters worse, the nation went from agricultural self-sufficiency to importing half its annual food needs as its farm output dropped steadily during the same period.[6]

These troubling developments provided the backdrop for the great depression of 1873, which was probably the single most important factor in sparking renewed interest in empire. Although crises of overproduction had beset the developing European industrial economies every seven to ten years in the preceding decades, the crash of 1873 was unprecedented in its scope and severity. Faced with dismal investment prospects, plummeting prices, and widespread unemployment, the industrial powers worried that their economies could grow no further. In Britain, panicked factory owners, financiers, and traders blamed the depression on the high tariff barriers of rival nations rather than admitting their inability to keep pace. Rejecting Adderley's warnings about the limited value of formal empire, they called for an expanded British imperial presence in tropical regions that were not yet open to western commerce and investment. Britain's continental rivals came to similar conclusions and rushed to reserve new African and Asian markets and sources of raw materials.

The subjugation of the East African highlands was part of this larger European conquest and partition of the African continent in the late nineteenth century. Historians lump this frenzy of empire building, along with the western powers' occupation of South Pacific islands, dismemberment of the Ottoman Empire, seizure of spheres of influence in China, and economic dominance of Latin America, under the heading of the "new imperialism." This global wave of imperial expansion was possible because the unifying power of nationalism and the industrial revolution gave westerners a relatively brief measure of military and commercial superiority over Africans and Asians.

Rather than being backward primitives, these new imperial victims were states and peoples whose sophistication, numbers, inhospitable climates, and/or geographical remoteness had spared them from early modern European empire building. In the late nineteenth century, ambitious European, American, and Japanese opportunists exploited these advantages to claim new empires and spheres of influence. For a brief window, permanent imperial rule once again appeared feasible and cost-effective in regions where the nation-state model had not yet taken hold.

Today, the new imperialism rivals Rome as the most popularly imagined model of empire, but the terms *new* and *imperialism* both require careful examination and explanation. The "old" imperialism referred to the American conquistador states and settlement colonies and the Asian chartered company empires of the early modern era. What was "new" about the conquest of the East African highlands was that it entailed the subjugation of the Nandi and other peoples who had escaped the first round of European imperial expansion but now lacked the means to deal with the growing power of the west. The discovery that quinine provided prophylactic protection from malaria allowed westerners to operate in tropical regions for extended periods, and repeating rifles, light field artillery, and the Maxim gun gave them the means to win inexpensive victories over much larger musket-equipped African armies. These advances made the new imperialism feasible by reducing the cost of conquest.

The new generation of late nineteenth-century imperial speculators first had to rehabilitate empire before they could exploit this imbalance. Imperial projects had a bad reputation in the mid-nineteenth-century western world after the devastation of the Napoleonic wars. Americans proudly imagined themselves as anti-imperial rebels, and in Europe Adderley and other liberals and free-traders dismissed empire as anachronistic and authoritarian. Indeed, the word *imperialism* first emerged as a pejorative synonym for *empire-building* when British critics coined it to attack Napoleon III's Second French Empire. In 1858, an anonymous article in the *Westminster Review* charged that in proclaiming himself emperor Napoleon's nephew aspired to "permanent military despotism," and the author quite correctly noted that "the permanent continuance of Imperialism resolves itself plainly into the establishment of undisguised military rule and the triumph of brute force."[7] *Imperialism* never lost

this negative meaning, particularly among twentieth-century critics of empire, but the imperial special-interest groups rehabilitated it in the 1880s by depicting empire as a profitable national enterprise.

Yet there were no more Bengals waiting to be conquered and exploited in the modern era. Partially commercialized African economies were poor outlets for western trade and investment, and J. A. Hobson, an imperial critic who covered the Anglo–South African War for the *Manchester Guardian*, was wrong in arguing that capitalist special interests sponsored the new wave of imperial expansion in Africa. In reality, British financiers put the bulk of their capital to work building railways and factories in the United States, Latin America, and Russia. The new imperialism stemmed primarily from fear and speculation, and only a small range of special-interest groups profited directly from the new empires. In addition to the merchants, missionaries, soldiers, and other men on the spot, these included the "gentlemanly capitalists" who controlled metropolitan banking, insurance, and shipping concerns.[8] Together, these latter-day nabobs exploited the temporary western advantage in technology, industry, and finance resulting from the uneven advance of globalization.

It is an open question as to how many people actually profited from the new imperialism. The overall value of the new empire to metropolitan Britain was certainly debatable. Britons at the turn of the twentieth century put 75 percent of their capital in nonimperial territories, and on average these investments brought approximately 1.58 percent higher returns than imperial ones.[9] For those willing to risk their money in the empire, India and the dominions remained the most lucrative outlets for trade and capital. The Raj was still unquestionably Britain's most valuable imperial possession. It offset Britain's trade imbalance with Europe, and the heavily subsidized Indian railways paid rich dividends to investors. The self-governing dominions were also important trading partners, but their value to Britain waned as they gained more control over their economies. By comparison, British Africa was nowhere near as valuable. The entire continent south of the Sahara took less than 5 percent of British exports in 1890, and when British capitalists did invest in the African empire they focused on the mines of southern Africa.[10] Lacking easily exploitable resources, sufficient infrastructure, and reliable labor supplies, the new protectorates were spectacularly poor investments, and the British government had to pay generous subsidies to draw capital to Africa.

Far from being a great engine of liberal free trade, this "new" British Empire was profoundly protectionist. Born of a deep sense of insecurity, it was Britain's desperate attempt to defend its global network of commerce and investment through non-economic means. Most British taxpayers probably would have preferred the cheaper option of informal empire, but the growing economic and military power of the United States, France, Germany, and to a lesser extent Russia and Japan scared the British government into indulging the imperial lobby's demands for more African and Asian territory. As a result, the British added almost five million square miles and ninety million more people to their formal empire in the last three decades of the nineteenth century. Although metropolitan Britain was a relatively small nation with a population of only forty-one and a half million, the new British Empire covered twelve million square miles (roughly one-quarter of the habitable world) and boasted more than four hundred million subjects at the turn of the twentieth century.[11]

As in the early modern era, bands of private explorers and chartered companies played the lead role in staking out claims to promising regions. In 1884, the European powers formalized this process at a conference in Berlin that the German chancellor Bismarck convened to ensure that squabbles over territory in Africa did not lead to war in Europe. In what amounted to the ground rules for the new imperialism, the delegates agreed that a nation wishing to claim a specific territory had to demonstrate that it occupied it "effectively." In practical terms, this meant direct administration and treaties in which the "natives" agreed to accept foreign protection. In many cases, the prominent local individuals who signed off on these protectorates did not realize that they were surrendering their sovereignty under European law. Instead, African leaders expected to be treated as equals and often hoped to use the foreigners against local rivals.

The British government was relatively restrained in this renewed rush for empire. In West Africa, it chartered Sir George Goldie's Royal Niger Company to claim Nigeria, but it only expanded territories surrounding the naval bases that Adderley wanted to give up. This is how the French came to claim most of West Africa. The central importance of India to the wider empire dictated the occupation of Egypt to safeguard the Suez Canal. Similarly, the Indian route around the Cape of Good Hope in southern Africa drew Britain into a war with the Transvaal and Orange Free State to ensure that

these mineral-rich Afrikaner republics did not swallow up the strategically important Cape Colony. Britain had no significant military or economic interests in central and eastern Africa, so the metropolitan government left the region to state-sanctioned private speculators. Thus, Cecil Rhodes's British South Africa Company claimed and conquered northern and southern Rhodesia, and Sir William McKinnon's British East Africa Company did the same in Uganda and the East African highlands.

Imperial enthusiasts swelled with pride in seeing these territories colored British pink, but metropolitan reactions to the new imperialism were decidedly mixed. Many Britons assumed that imperialism meant building closer ties with the white settlement colonies and not the conquest of alien and inassimilable Africans and Asians. While Rhodes, Meinertzhagen, and other adventurers made fortunes and careers in the new territories, more often than not the British taxpayer paid for their empires. The Treasury was particularly suspicious of the new imperialism and criticized the expense of unnecessary imperial wars. The imperial special interests countered by appealing to the public's patriotic and humanitarian sentiments. Popular newspapers depicted the new empire as a heroic national enterprise, and music hall shows carried the message to the working classes. Rudyard Kipling, Rider Haggard, John Buchan, and other widely read authors spun romantic tales of adventure and national glory in the empire.

The resulting wave of popular enthusiasm generated by this celebration of empire meant that there was very little real political debate over the nature and merits of the new imperialism. Liberal and Tory politicians argued over its particulars, but both parties recognized the power of popular imperial sentiment. Benjamin Disraeli argued that the empire made Britain great, and Lord Randolph Churchill and Joseph Chamberlain courted working-class voters by promising that the new conquests provided markets and new lands for settlement. Alternatively, William Gladstone, H. H. Asquith, and other Liberals appealed to the public's better nature by depicting the new empire as benevolent.

While this imperial expansion might appear inevitable in hindsight, it caught nonwestern peoples almost entirely by surprise. For nearly four centuries, coastal Africans interacted with Europeans as trading partners and allies in struggles with rival neighbors. Slave traders were certainly a threat, but on balance most African societies

of ivory. Additionally, the British abolitionists' success in outlawing the Atlantic slave trade had the unexpected consequence of pushing human trafficking into Central and East Africa. This was the result of a loophole that the British government inserted into the antislavery treaties to allow their Portuguese allies to buy and capture slaves south of the equator. Led by Afro-Arab adventurers and bankrolled by Indian investors, armed caravans hunted elephants and people in the highlands. Captured slaves carried the tusks to the coast, where these speculators doubled their profits by selling both commodities. Most of the ivory was destined for western markets, and the slaves went to Zanzibari plantations, the Middle East, and Brazil, where slavery remained legal until the 1880s.

These caravans integrated the highlands into the wider networks of trade and investment. Less advantageous, they spread firearms and contagious diseases. Merchant adventurers such as Tippu Tib carved out minor empires in the interior, and young highlanders who acquired guns to hunt elephants joined caravan deserters and runaway slaves in preying on local communities. This explains why Richard Burton, David Livingstone, and other explorers and missionaries encountered anarchy and violence when they mapped these regions at midcentury. Assuming that slave raiding, warfare, famine, and widespread misery were endemic, they had little clue that western demands for ivory and the misguided efforts of the humanitarian lobby were at the root of many of these problems.

This ignorance allowed the missionaries and fortune seekers who followed the explorers to portray Africans as primitive and in need of rescue and salvation. The metropolitan government initially paid little attention to these special interests. It saw no value in East Africa during the era of informal empire, and it took the threat of German expansion into the great lakes region to spur Prime Minister Lord Salisbury into action in the 1880s. Motivated by an unrealistic fear that a foreign presence on Lake Victoria/Nyanza and the headwaters of the Nile would threaten British control of Egypt and the Suez Canal, Salisbury's government chartered Sir William MacKinnon's IBEAC to stake a formal claim to the highlands. From the British government's standpoint, MacKinnon's enterprise was a cost effective way to establish "effective administration" of the northern end of the highlands under the terms of the Berlin Conference. Germany claimed what became modern Tanzania, and Britain acquired control

could deal with Europeans on relatively equal terms before the industrial era. Even more troubling, the new imperialism stripped them of their humanity.

Seeking to lend credence to their promise to civilize the "primitive races" of Africa, imperial speculators and their mission allies portrayed subject peoples as implicitly and often irredeemably backward. Most missionaries genuinely believed that the imperial wars of conquest were liberating, but the popular theories of social Darwinism and pseudoscientific racism, which depicted nonwesterners as biologically inferior, gave this seemingly benevolent imperial project an inherently sinister reality. While late nineteenth-century western intellectuals and politicians cited the unique characteristics of the British, French, and German "races" in making national distinctions, they placed all Europeans on a scale of cultural evolution far above the supposedly backward overseas peoples. Ethnographers and scientists confidently found evidence of this primitiveness by using comparative anatomy and craniology to prove that nonwestern peoples had smaller brains and diminished cognitive ability. E. S. Grogan, one of the most grasping new Kenyan imperialists, blithely declared that it was "patent to all who have observed the African native, that he is fundamentally inferior in mental development and ethical possibilities (call it a soul if you will) to the white man."12

Consequently, by the late nineteenth century it was no longer possible to be African and civilized within the British Empire. Africans became people without history, people who lived in timeless and unchanging backward tribal societies. This meant that westernized communities such as the Sierra Leonean Krios, who ran Britain's West African coastal enclaves, became "trousered natives" who, like the Indian baboos, aped a modern culture they did not understand. It did not matter that many were graduates of British universities, or that Samuel Adjai Crowther was an Anglican bishop and James Africanus Horton was a British army doctor. The new pseudoscientific racism created a liberal excuse for empire by turning all darkcomplected peoples into primitives.

This was the grim scenario that played out in East Africa. Highland peoples, who traded with coastal Swahili city states through middlemen, became more directly integrated into global trade networks in the early nineteenth century when western middle-class demand for combs, piano keys, and billiard balls drove up the price

over Zanzibar and, by extension, the Kenyan coastline by forcing the sultan to accept British "protection."

MacKinnon had vague but ambitious plans to develop the region and depicted his holdings as a "new Australia." But his company soon teetered on bankruptcy because the region lacked exploitable mineral resources and its local economies were not suited to easy extraction. Few East Africans in the interior produced commodities for the world market, which meant that MacKinnon could not emulate Clive's success in India by capturing preexisting trade and tax systems. To make matters worse, his charter required him to occupy the lake kingdom of Buganda at considerable expense. MacKinnon's only hope of survival was a government subsidy for a railway linking Mombasa to the highlands, but his enterprise was doomed once the Liberal prime minister William Gladstone refused to saddle the British taxpayer with such an expensive enterprise.

MacKinnon was a prototypical example of a failed imperial speculator. Although he benefited from western advances in commerce and technology, he had no means of extracting wealth from his new subjects. Many of his original employees were trained geologists, but their desperate search for economically viable mineral deposits was fruitless. Realizing that custom duties on the caravan trade were the region's only significant revenue source, MacKinnon essentially took over the old Afro-Arab trade network. His caravans employed many of the same coastal peoples who had initially chartered the highland trade, although they no longer engaged in slave raiding and elephant hunting.

Given these realities, it is hardly surprising that the IBEAC had difficulty attracting investors. Handicapped by a chronic capital shortage, MacKinnon lacked the means to govern and develop the highlands. He escaped total ruin when the more imperially minded prime minister Lord Rosebery claimed the Uganda and East Africa Protectorates in 1894 and 1895 on the assumption that the source of the Nile had sufficient strategic importance to warrant the expense of direct intervention. Having bought out MacKinnon and his investors, Rosebery concluded that the Treasury would have to take financial responsibility for replacing the caravan route from Mombasa to Uganda with a railway. In investing some nine million pounds of state funds in the project, he implicitly committed the British government to completing the IBEAC's conquest of East Africa. MacKinnon was

off the hook, and most of his employees continued their careers in government service.

The Foreign Office had responsibility for the new protectorates until the Colonial Office took them over in 1906. This fit the overall pattern for the new British Empire. Administratively, the Crown was the source of executive authority in every British-controlled territory, but in practice there was no uniform or integrated system of governance. In London, a variety of government ministries instead shared responsibility for imperial oversight. The Foreign Office initially ran most of the African protectorates, but as in East Africa, it handed off most of these territories to the Colonial Office. The India Office oversaw the Raj and an extensive Indian Civil Service that was separate and distinct from the rest of the colonial service. In practical terms, however, the Treasury exercised the greatest influence of all the metropolitan ministries because the chancellors of the Exchequer stood in the way of speculators who sought to shift the costs of empire to the metropolitan government. The British East Africa Company was a notable exception to this rule.

Otherwise, the EAP followed the standard imperial template by dividing the newly conquered territory into provinces, districts, and African "locations." The Protestant missions adopted a similar strategy in apportioning the protectorate into spheres of influence to ensure that they did not compete with each other. In terms of governance, a commissioner, whose title later became governor, presided over a central secretariat, several specialized departments, and the larger field administration. These district officers supervised the chiefs who actually ruled the African majority under the doctrine of indirect rule.

In pretending to rule through local sovereigns, the British imported the Indian model of imperial rule to Africa. As in the Raj, British officials claimed to govern through African institutions of authority rather than ruling directly. This made the "tribe" the basis of imperial administration. Confused by the range of fluid and often overlapping ethnicities of preconquest Africa, British officials concluded that Africans lived in unchanging tribal societies. In the imperial imagination, a tribe was a lower form of political and social organization that, with proper paternal guidance, might one day evolve into a nation. Theoretically, these tribal identities were biologically ingrained, thereby making them fixed and corporate rather than individual. Working in the service of colonial governments, anthropologists mapped tribal languages, social institutions, and customary laws to fashion the tools of imperial administration for district officers. The African tribe was thus a useful fiction to update the venerable imperial strategy of co-opting local institutions of authority. This indirect rule lowered the cost of administration and allowed the new imperialists to portray themselves as philosopher-kings in the Platonic tradition.

However, British officials actually knew very little about the local institutions and customs they claimed to protect. Their ignorance created opportunities for ambitious individuals to convince imperial officials and ethnographers to make them chiefs with useful vested authority to define the tribal customs that became the basis of imperial administration. As John Iliffe famously noted: "Europeans believed Africans belonged to tribes; Africans built tribes to belong to," and the origins of the Mijikenda, Kalenjin, Luhya and other contemporary Kenyan "tribes" date from the imperial era.[13] The opportunities of imperially defined tribalism thus encouraged subject peoples to frame political and social debates in tribal terms. In doing so, they played into the hands of the new imperialists, for tribal status disqualified Africans from membership in the British nation-state. Metropolitan Britons were technically "subjects" of the British Crown, but in practice they were citizens with the full rights and protections of British law. Tribal Africans, conversely, were "protected persons," with no individual rights. Instead of citizenship, the British imperial system granted collective rights to tribes.

The complication was that while indirect rule worked relatively well in the Raj, where sultans and maharajas had substantial authority, these Indian rulers had few counterparts in sub-Saharan Africa. where, like the Nandi, most societies were stateless. This meant that there were multiple sites of authority in a given community and no single individual had the power to govern autonomously, collect taxes, or rule on "native law." In most territories, British officials compensated by turning cooperative individuals with some measure of influence into "chiefs." But this was not the equivalent of Napoleonic *ralliement*, for few of these men were true local notables. Similarly, imperial administrators solved the problem of statelessness by lumping related communities together into tribes under the nominal authority of these imperial proxies. While it did not have the power to force Africans to accept these tribal identities, the imperial regime

created a powerful incentive for them to think tribally by refusing to acknowledge them as individuals. Tellingly, individualistic western-educated Africans such as the Sierra Leonean Krios had to be shunted aside because they were too individualistic and "modern."

It took some time for the Nandi and the rest of the highland communities to realize the consequences of these developments. Peoples living along the route to Lake Nyanza/Victoria, which IBEAC officials called the Buganda Road, saw both danger and opportunity in the expanding British presence. Initially, there were profits to be made by supplying the company with food, water, and labor. In the central highlands, a Kikuyu trader named Kinyanjui made himself useful by provisioning the caravans. Likewise, Mumia, a relatively minor Luhya clan leader on the northern shore of Lake Victoria/Nyanza, used his connections with the company to become a powerful chief. At the same time, MacKinnon's men also provoked highland communities when they resorted to foraging, which was essentially looting, to the expense of bartering supplies. That there were no rich treasures to plunder in the highlands did not mean that these latter-day conquistadors were any more virtuous than their predecessors.

Koitalel's followers and other young warriors who had no stake in commerce further hindered the company's ability to turn a profit. Preferring raiding to trading, they made the caravans' long trek from Mombasa to Buganda difficult and dangerous. Indian work gangs building the Uganda Railway were similarly at risk. The company initially dealt with this threat by fortifying its food stations, but the Foreign Office, which had little patience for local interference with a multimillion-pound construction project, adopted a more aggressive response. It reorganized the private company army into the KAR to bolster British authority in the new protectorates. This "native force" reduced the cost of empire by following the chartered company practice of recruiting ex-slaves and other poorly paid marginal peoples for service against more established communities.

Led by seconded regular army officers such as Richard Meinertzhagen, the KAR companies, backed by "native auxiliaries" and Indian troops on loan from the Raj, gradually forced the peoples of the highlands to accept imperial subjecthood. For the first decade of its existence the EAP's main business was conquest. From 1895 to 1905, the total cost of these pacification campaigns came to more than six thousand pounds, which was one-third of the protectorate's total expenditures.[14] The operations that led to Meinertzhagen's execution of Koitalel were fairly typical. Often devolving into mass cattle raids, these small but vicious wars usually ended when protectorate troops forced defiant communities to surrender by seizing their livestock and burning their huts and crops.

The resulting famines contributed to the devastatingly high mortality rates that afflicted the highlands at the end of the nineteenth century. Racked by hunger and epidemic disease, weakened East Africans struggled to cope with the British invasion. Once again, smallpox in particular played a central role in western empire building. Spread by the caravans along with cholera, pneumonia, and other deadly pathogens, it ravaged communities whose relative isolation in the highlands made them dangerously vulnerable to contagious Old World diseases. Rinderpest, a highly virulent cattle disease originating in South Asia, and bovine pleuropneumonia (lungsickness) made matters even worse by wiping out the herds that were both a food source and a measure of wealth. Estimates vary, but it appears that these human and biological disasters may have killed off as much as 30 to 50 percent of the population of the central and northern highlands.[15]

Although there were a few exceptions, the Nandi surrender in 1905 generally marked the end of open African resistance. With British rule secure, the pacification operations that brought glory to Meinertzhagen and other ambitious empire builders now became an expensive embarrassment and hindered the process of orderly extraction. As one of his fellow officers in the King's African Rifles candidly acknowledged, it was no longer "the object of the KAR to kill potential British subjects, especially as they are expected to become tax-payers and profitable customers."[16]

As with earlier empires, the imperial regime viewed the East Africans primarily as exploitable subjects rather than consumers. Anxious to recoup the nine million pounds that metropolitan taxpayers had invested in the Uganda Railway, protectorate authorities cast about for paying passengers and shippers. Giving far too much credibility to the denigrating ideologies of empire building, they failed to realize that many African farmers gladly would have produced crops for export if given sufficient access to global markets via the railway. Instead, the EAP's commissioner, Sir Charles Eliot, concluded that it would take a civilized people to develop the highlands. As the line

neared completion in 1903, imperial officials considered and dismissed Indian peasants, Afrikaner homesteaders, and even Theodor Herzl's Zionists before committing themselves to enticing aristocratic Britons to settle in East Africa.

Building this elite settler society took some doing, for the pioneer empire builders in East Africa were anything but noble. As in the early stages of most imperial projects, the protectorate tended to attract marginal men and fortune hunters. They were a sorry collection of adventurers, hunters, con men, drunkards, and outright criminals who were hardly the best representatives of the civilized west. Slipping the bonds of metropolitan conceptions of morality, they had free rein to indulge their lust for wealth and power. Bartolomé de Las Casas, Edmund Burke, and other earlier metropolitan critics of empire would have recognized these corrupting imperial influences. Meinertzhagen at least was honest about how serving the East Africa Protectorate tested him.

It is hard to resist the savagery of Africa when one falls under its spell. One soon reverts to one's ancestral character, both mind and temperament becoming brutalized. I have seen so much of it out here and I have myself felt the magnetic power of the African climate drawing me lower and lower to the level of a savage.[17]

In his eyes, most KAR officers were "regimental rejects" who failed this test by becoming obsessed with money, drink, pornography, mistresses, and small boys.[18] Precious few of the men who did the messy work of empire building were suited to be capitalist entrepreneurs or sober landed gentlemen, and migrants leaving Britain with agricultural experience had far better options in the United States and the dominions. Apart from about 280 itinerant Afrikaners from the Transvaal, there were only one hundred permanent settlers in the protectorate in 1903.

Eliot therefore recognized that it would take significant inducements to lure the right kind of men to East Africa. Seizing land from the Maasai, Kikuyu, Nandi, Kamba, and other highland communities, he offered settlers ninety-nine-year leases on parcels of 640 acres of prime agricultural land at the rock-bottom rate of less than one pence per acre. Companies could apply for even larger concessions ranging up to one hundred thousand acres, and a new ordinance in 1915 increased the tenure of the leases to 999 years. Even these generous

made ideal customers for the Uganda Railway. Company agents at the time described the Kikuyu heartland as "one vast garden," and even Johnston's comrade Frederick Lugard had to admit that their "whole country may be said to be under tillage."[21]

The Maasai, by comparison, found another way to recover from the disasters of the previous decade. Finding common cause with the British invaders, they rebuilt their herds by enlisting as native auxiliaries in the pacification campaigns. While postindependence Kenyan nationalists might have viewed this as treason, East Africans had no reason to identify themselves collectively, much less nationally, until the imperial era. From the Maasai standpoint, the IBEAC was a useful ally in their struggle with far more threatening rivals such as the Nandi and Kikuyu. They had no reason to suspect that British settlers would eventually displace them by claiming three-quarters of the Rift Valley.

This is why the totality of the imperial conquest shocked most communities. In just a few decades, the British made a quick transition from useful trading partners and political allies to plundering but manageable marauders and then to determined land-stealing empire builders. The father of political activist Harry Thuku was stunned to find that a government official suddenly claimed title to his farm, and he had little recourse when the Europeans told him: "You have no land. The land belongs to God. God has given it to the white man, and they have it now."[22] Just as Iberians and Andeans turned to prophecy to explain the totality of their defeat, East Africans now recalled the warnings of oracles and wise men who foretold the arrival of the pale-skinned foreigners and their railway. The Nandi remembered that Koitalel's father, Kimnyole, had prophesized that whites borne by a giant shrieking, crawling, and smoking serpent would come to kill his sons, take their cattle, and drive them from their homes. The Kikuyu recorded that Mogo wa Kebiro issued similar warnings about strangers colored like frogs and bearing magical fire-belching sticks.[23] These tales were not the result of primitive superstition; they were born of the highland communities' desperate need to make sense of their enormous losses.

In time, their children recognized the conquest for the imperial power grab that it really was. Writing three decades later, Jomo Kenyatta blamed the Kikuyu defeat on their willingness to befriend the European strangers who appeared in the country as tired and

inducements did not bring the expected rush of settlers, and land speculation proved far more profitable than farming. By the opening of the First World War, less than 10 percent of the alienated land was under cultivation, but farms that went for six pence per acre in 1903 were selling for one pound per acre in 1914. Moreover, powerful imperial interests and syndicates used political and family connections to buy up much of the available land. This gave five individuals and two syndicates the means to acquire 20 percent of the highlands, and in 1912 there were still only about one thousand permanent settlers in the protectorate.[19]

The imperial regime's legal authority for this blatant land theft was the Crown Lands Ordinance of 1902, which gave the Crown title to all "unoccupied" land in the protectorate. Linking land and identity, this legislation also set up a "native reserve" for each tribe. Theoretically, these reservations prevented unscrupulous European or South Asian speculators from duping ignorant tribesmen into selling lands that were their tribe's communal property. As one official paternalistically claimed, the Crown's ownership of African land was a legal fiction intended to "protect the natives from themselves." This was nonsense, and in reality the actual purpose of the reserve system was to open up the protectorate for expropriation by Europeans. The highlands thus became the "white highlands," which developed into a three-million-hectare settler "native" reserve off-limits to Africans. The peoples of the coast and the western Lake Nyanza/Victoria region did not lose land directly to western settlement, but they too became subject natives.

Imperial officials tried to legitimize these land seizures by depicting the highlands as underpopulated. Sir Harry Johnston described them as "admirably suited for a white man's country" because they were "utterly uninhabited for miles or at most its inhabitants are wandering hunters who have no settled home."[20] In fact, most highland communities were well on the way to demographic recovery from the devastation of the 1890s by the time Eliot began to promote European settlement. The Kikuyu in particular expanded rapidly during this period by sending landless young men to carve out new farms on the margins of their territory. British demands for food for caravan porters, railway laborers, and settlers accelerated this process by giving entrepreneurial Kikuyu farmers an incentive to increase their agricultural output. Ironically, these ambitious men would have

hungry vagrants and wanderers. Assuming that these people would be temporary sojourners, the Kikuyu elders signed their treaties and granted them permission to settle temporarily as clients. In Kenyatta's view, his people were defeated through treachery, not because they were somehow culturally inferior. "The Gikuyu lost their lands through their magnanimity, for the Gikuyu country was never wholly conquered by force of arms, but the people were put under the ruthless domination of European imperialism through the insidious trickery of hypocritical treaties."[24]

Protectorate officials and settlers dismissed or muzzled this opposition by portraying East Africans as primitive tribesmen lacking the capacity to make proper use of the rich highlands. But the EAP also struggled to attract the right kind of settler. Anxious to be rid of the politically embarrassing lumpen rabble that had undertaken the original conquest of the highlands, Eliot was determined to make the protectorate an aristocratic "white man's country."

The commissioner had an ally in Lord Cranworth, a member of the House of Lords with extensive interests in East Africa, who published a book promoting the EAP as the perfect place for English elites to create the feudal society of privilege and deference that they believed had withered away in democratic industrial Britain. With chapters on health, climate, agriculture, animal husbandry, hunting, horse racing, polo, and other sporting pursuits, the book claimed that the protectorate had everything a propertied Englishman could want.

A perfect balmy climate? Take Nairobi and Kyambu. Something a little more bracing and with a touch of frost? Try Likipia or the Uasin Gishu plateau. Would you have a reminder of the West coast of Scotland with heavy rain, mist and lovely days interspersed? The Mau or the Nandi Escarpment will give it [to] you. A touch of the wind off the North Sea in East Anglia? The West Kenia plains can do that. While something really cold and bitter you must climb up into Kenia's glaciers.[25]

This sort of advertising drew men like Hugh Cholmondeley (Lord Delamere), who purchased one hundred thousand acres in the highlands for just five thousand pounds at the tender age of twenty-eight. Strict immigration controls required would-be immigrants to prove they had at least one thousand pounds in the bank, and the government deported to Bombay poorer undesirables who might diminish

"white prestige" after first forcing them to work off the cost of their passage in the Mombasa jail.[26]

Although they had no formal position of authority in the EAP, Delamere and the settler aristocracy had considerable influence over sympathetic protectorate officials. In 1907, they won the right to elect representatives to the Legislative Council, and their Convention of Associations became a virtual lower parliamentary house. Opened by the governor (formerly the protectorate commissioner), the convention called officials to testify on government policy and debated bills under consideration in the formal legislative council.

Nevertheless, the settlers never felt physically or morally secure. Although they had their own militia, they relied on the European-led African soldiers of the KAR and "native" policemen for their protection. Those living on remote farms worried constantly about their safety, particularly when the press carried a report or rumor of an African assault on a European. The fact that these "outrages" were actually extremely rare was not reassuring. Ever mindful that they were a privileged minority, the settler community relied on the illusion of racial and cultural superiority to exercise authority. This is why Grogan insisted that European prestige "must be maintained at all costs, as it is the sole hold we have over the native."[27] Strict racial segregation concealed the settlers' inherent vulnerability, and they strove futilely to create all-white enclaves where Africans would only visit as domestic servants and temporary laborers.

The settlers staked their claim to the highlands by asserting that they alone had the means to develop the protectorate, but African produce accounted for 70 percent of the EAP's exports before the First World War. The settlers nevertheless justified their privileges by depicting Africans as irredeemably simple and slothful. The Kikuyu came in for particular abuse as the settlers' chief agricultural and political rivals, and Cranworth unashamedly described them as "a most miserable cowardly race."[28] This was empire at its most hypocritical, for Cranworth's estates would have been worthless without Kikuyu to work them.

As in earlier empires, the East Africa Protectorate's true wealth was in its people. The settlers reconciled their labor demands with the imperial lobby's humanitarian rhetoric by depicting toil as inherently civilizing. Frederick Lugard, Britain's foremost imperial ideologue, reassured the metropolitan public that it was possible to both uplift Africa's "native races" and exploit its resources. He asserted that the "white races" had a moral obligation to make the continent's wealth available to the wider world by directing their labor.[29] Invoking Lugard's declaration of this "dual mandate," the colonial secretary Leopold Amery confidently told the Houses of Commons: "Our first duty is to [our African subjects]; our object is not to exploit them, but to enable them materially, as well as in every other respect, to rise to a high plane of living and civilization."[30]

Rhetoric aside, the fortunes of settler farmers, concession holders, and speculators depended on a poorly paid, subservient African work force. Most westerners came to East Africa with the expectation that Africans would grow their food, build their houses, and tend to their most basic domestic needs. In the settlers' eyes, the EAP was obliged to supply this cheap if not free labor. The complication was that the moral veneer of the new imperialism prevented the EAP from simply forcing Africans to work. Eliot and his successors came under considerable criticism for taking their time in abolishing slavery on the Swahili coast. Unwilling to disrupt the relatively lucrative plantation economy, they tried to extend the immoral institution's life by pretending that it would gradually die out on its own accord. Realistically, slavery was no longer a viable tool of imperial extraction, and settlers and speculators had to find more civilized ways to harness African labor.

Initially, however, most East Africans had little incentive to work on imperial enterprises because their subsistence economies met most of their needs. Those that did accept paid employment usually did so just long enough to earn enough money to buy useful western material goods such as clothing, cutlery, or bicycles before returning home. Frustrated would-be employers therefore charged that Africans were inherently lazy. A settler newspaper published an unflinchingly racist poem that typified this view of African men as indolent, unmanly drunkards who lived off the labor of their wives.

Jack Nigger you're as cute's can be
Five beans to you make ten
You drink and scrounge and sleep and laze
And laze, scrounge and drink again!
Your bibis [wives] do domestic jobs
They sow and plough and reap
And mend your pants and mind the kids
While you lie fast asleep.

In fact they live for you alone
You gay and lazy dog
They make and fetch your pombe [beer] and
They feed you like a hog
And with it all but one thing can
Disturb your lordly rest
And that, Jack Nig, you likewise know
Is twenty of the best.[31]

The phrase "twenty of the best" referred to flogging. Far from being embarrassed by the settlers' extensive use of corporal punishment, a member of the Kenyan Legislative Council unashamedly declared in open debate: "I always treat my natives the same as I treat children. I try to be kind to them, and to advise and direct them, but when kindness has no effect you have to do the same as they do in the public schools at home and throughout the empire—use the cane."[32] Exempted from western conceptions of morality and the rule of law by virtue of their race, the settlers sometimes beat their employees to death while teaching the value of "honest" work. The early years of British rule in Kenya were so corrupting that even Norman Leys, a vehement critic of the settlers, admitted that he too gave in to the seductive power of the racialized new imperialism. "You see I have lived in the fog myself. I have cuffed and kicked boys [Africans], sometimes because for the moment it seemed that [in no way] else could things be done, sometimes because my mind was tired beyond control, sometimes because I hated the people I kicked, though I never hated them as I hated myself."[33]

The protectorate government therefore cast about for more politically acceptable ways to produce African labor. The most obvious answer was to destroy local subsistence economies. On the whole, simple taxation proved the most effective strategy. The protectorate's relatively meager gross tax receipts were quiet small, but introducing the poll and hut tax, with mandatory payments in rupees and later shillings, required East Africans to find paying jobs. By 1910, they had to pay Rs 3 for each hut and Rs 3 for the individual poll tax each year. Defaulters lost their huts and crops and had to work one month for each rupee owed.[34] Europeans, in turn, did not pay a direct income tax until the late 1930s, leaving their "native" subjects to fund the settlers' schools, hospitals, and other amenities.

Africans could have raised their tax money by selling crops and livestock, but the native reserve system created land shortages that made it difficult to produce for the market. This meant that men and women had to sell their labor to avoid breaking the law. This subtle form of imperial coercion was both inexpensive and acceptable to the humanitarian lobby for all "civilized" people had to pay taxes. In the EAP, however, civilized people did not have an obligation to pay a fair wage. Desperate to keep the labor costs down, settlers and speculators used their influence to depress African pay scales. But even minimal wages were sufficient for most Africans to cover their taxes, which meant that most still avoided wage labor whenever they could. Moreover, the tendency of some of the EAP's poorly made coins to literally disintegrate when exposed to the elements hardly inspired confidence in the cash economy.

European employers therefore used every political resource at their disposal to press the EAP to institute a comprehensive program of forced labor. The settlers never got the government to recruit workers for them directly, but the imperial regime ordered district officers and chiefs to compel Africans to build roads, dams, and irrigation systems. These forced laborers even had to carry administrative officials on litters through the largely roadless rural areas. The EAP also turned a relatively blind eye to the abuses of unscrupulous private labor recruiters who used coercion and deception to get laborers to sign exploitive contracts. Those who ran away from abusive employers faced prosecution under a Master and Servants Ordinance. In 1912, reports of these excesses forced protectorate authorities to commission an investigation of "native labour" that acknowledged that chiefs and labor recruiters were forcing people to work by burning their huts, seizing their land, and fining them excessively.

The First World War only made matters worse. Dominating the protectorate war council, the settlers won new authority to round up laborers under martial law regulations by depicting African resistance to wage labor as traitorous. Even worse, the military authorities demanded huge numbers of men to support the largely futile three-year invasion of German East Africa (modern Tanzania). British, Indian, and South African troops initially took the lead in the operation, but mounting loses due to combat and disease led imperial generals to rely on local African troops. The East Africa, Uganda, and Nyasaland protectorates supplied more than thirty thousand African

soldiers for the King's African Rifles during the campaign, but this paled in comparison to the hundreds of thousands of laborers the civil authorities conscripted to carry supplies. Recordkeeping from this era is poor, but it appears that at least fifty thousand of these "carriers" perished as a result of combat, disease, and gross mistreatment during the East African campaign.

The imperial authorities refused to even acknowledge African contributions to Britain's victory. Instead, the protectorate government seized half a million more acres of Nandi and Kikuyu land in 1919 to provide farms for demobilized British military officers. Designed to strengthen white settlement, the Soldier Settlement Scheme opened 685 new farms to qualified applicants of pure European origin with demonstrated assets worth at least one thousand pounds. A supplementary plan set aside additional land and one hundred thousand pounds for disabled veterans to grow flax. Precious few of the soldier settlers had any agricultural experience and most sold out to land speculators within a few short years. The participants in the flax scheme went bankrupt when global prices for the commodity crashed.

In 1920, the metropolitan government acknowledged the settlers' preeminent place in East Africa by transforming the EAP into the Kenya Colony and Protectorate. Most settlers expected this to set Kenya on the path to self-government and possibly even dominion status. They elected two representatives to the governor's Executive Council, which served as his cabinet. Their representatives in the Legislative Council had a majority on the Finance Committee and took a more direct role in drafting laws. A series of pro-settler governors worked closely with these "unofficial" elected legislators and often signed off on laws without sending them on to the Colonial Office for formal approval. A Chief Native Commissioner supposedly spoke for the African majority in the Executive Council, while a single appointed missionary represented "native" interests in the legislature.

Imperial apologists argued that tribal Africans were not sufficiently educated to speak for themselves. Not only was this absurd, it was also hypocritical. The imperial regime had no intention of giving its subjects the western-style education that was a prerequisite for the franchise. In 1924, the Kenyan government spent just 4 percent of its seventy-five-thousand pound education budget on African children.[35]

Apart from a few government schools, the Education Department left "native education" almost entirely in the hands of the missions, which were so powerful in East Africa that the evolutionary biologist Julian Huxley, who became an expert on imperial education, labeled them a "de facto Third Estate."

While the missions helped legitimize British imperial rule through their evangelical efforts, their schools served the equally important role of training the inexpensive African clerks, tradesmen, and skilled laborers that made indirect rule economically feasible. As the labor expert William Ormsby-Gore acknowledged: "The economic development of tropical Africa calls increasingly for Africans to man the railways, the motor lorries, to build, to carpenter, and to do a thousand things which are familiar to us and quite new and strange to the African."[26] At the same time, British administrators never forgot that Thomas Babington Macaulay's attempt to create a loyal western-educated class of Indians that was "English in taste, in opinions, in morals, and in intellect" helped produce the Indian National Congress. Anxious to avoid repeating that mistake in Africa, they sought to make Africans "better natives" by teaching them to respect manual labor and tribal chiefly authority instead of aspiring to be "black Europeans." As a babooist Tanganyikan official sneeringly observed: "Does anyone who sees the Europeanised African believe him to be genuine? Too often he seems only a caricature of a European and an insult to his own race."[37] The Colonial Office's Advisory Committee on Native Education in British Tropical Africa therefore embraced the southern American states' segregated industrial education model in the hope of training skilled laborers without also producing political agitators.

In Kenya, the Anglican and Presbyterian missions shared these views, but they were also reasonably committed to offering advanced schooling for at least some of their students. The Catholic Church and the heavily evangelical African Inland Mission, however, believed that their converts needed only a basic level of literacy to read the Bible. The resulting narrow educational pyramid denied African communities a political voice and ensured that they had to speak through chiefs and tribal representatives.

Comparatively speaking, the immigrant South Asian community was a much more serious threat to settler dominance in East Africa. Outnumbering Europeans by more than two to one in the interwar

era, the approximately thirty-eight thousand Asians demanded equal political representation and permission to buy farms in the white highlands.[38] Although they had few legal rights, they had considerable economic influence in Kenya because long-standing and extensive commercial ties throughout the Indian Ocean allowed them to mobilize capital much more easily than the settlers could. They were the real driving force behind the growth of Nairobi, and a railway contractor named A. M. Jivanjee was one of the city's largest landowners in the 1920s.

The Asian challenge led the settlers to push for strict immigration limits and a formal declaration from the metropolitan government that Kenya was indeed a "white man's country." In doing so they overreached themselves, for the interwar Colonial Office was less sympathetic to their agenda. In 1923 the colonial secretary, Lord Devonshire, issued a white paper formally declaring that African interests in Kenya were "paramount" over those of both the British and Indian "immigrant races." The settlers were predictably outraged, and an extreme faction went so far as to hatch a ridiculous conspiracy for an armed uprising. They actually had little to worry about. Devonshire's declaration effectively blocked Asian expansion in Kenya, and a subsequent 1927 white paper affirmed the settlers' right to share in the "responsibilities of government" by declaring that Africans were best served by avoiding "clashes of interest" with the European community.

Assured that Kenya was a country for white men, the most ambitious imperial partisans dreamed of an East African Federation comprising Kenya, Uganda, and Tanganyika (the former German East Africa). Africans in the other two territories saw this as a bid by the Kenyan settlers for control of the entire East African highlands. "Natives" had no voice in high imperial policy, but the Ugandans and Tanganyikans were fortunate that the plan floundered with the depression.

Realistically, the imperial special interests were in no position to sustain an East African Federation. Large plantations on the coast brought the Kenyan government some revenue through export tariffs, but the neomercantilist nature of the new imperialism effectively ruled out industrial development in the colony. The Colonial Office blocked a bid by Asian entrepreneurs to build a textile mill, to ensure it did not compete with metropolitan weavers, and most manufacturing enterprises involved the production of soap, flour, fats, jam, tobacco, and beer for local consumption. The Magadi Soda Ash Company, which was Kenya's only viable export industry, needed a subsidized railway branch line simply to stay in business. In many years the metropolitan Treasury had to help balance the colony's budget, which demonstrated that the British government had made a particularly poor investment in choosing the settlers to drive Kenya's economic development. Most were inept farmers who spent most of their income on creature comforts instead of improving production. They depended on short-term loans to finance future plantings but had difficulty establishing good credit because speculation drove the value of their land beyond its actual capacity.

High production costs meant that the settlers needed protective tariffs, reduced railway rates, and extremely cheap labor to remain competitive. Securing abundant supplies of African labor was the most viable of the three strategies, for the Congo Basin Treaty limited the Kenyan government's ability to restrict trade. Furthermore, the Uganda government refused to pay higher freight costs on imports to subsidize Kenyan exports. The settlers therefore returned to the prewar strategy of trying to turn their political influence to extractive ends. In addition to demanding government assistance in labor recruiting, they also wanted higher African taxes, restrictive employment laws, and permission to forcibly discipline their workers.

While the Kenyan imperial authorities were sympathetic, coerced labor in any form was politically indefensible in interwar Britain. In 1919, settler leaders convinced Governor Sir Edward Northey to issue a series of circular orders directing district officers to "exercise every possible lawful influence" in pushing African men, women, and even children to "come out into the labour field." The first and most controversial circular warned that the government would have to resort to "special methods" if particular communities did not produce sufficient numbers of workers. Intense metropolitan criticism forced Northey to issue a follow-up order clarifying that he did not expect government officials to recruit labor directly for private employers. Instead he increased the African poll tax from ten shillings to sixteen and pointed out that while "no actual force can be employed to compel a man to go out to work, he can, however, be made to pay his tax." The unspoken assumption in this statement was that defaulters would work for the settlers. Finally, the governor took the particular

controversial step of making wage labor a greater priority than work on African peasant farms, which raised the risk of famine in many communities.[39] Northey, who, as a native-born South African, was particularly sympathetic to settler interests, was uncompromising in removing district officers who balked at implementing the circulars.

The Conservative imperial enthusiast Leopold Amery defended Northey's actions in Parliament by claiming that they would save East Africans from dying out like the Amerindians and Polynesians. This argument carried little weight with the humanitarian lobby. While this coalition of missionaries, antislavery activists, liberal civil servants, and socialists generally agreed with Northey that Africans should work, they absolutely rejected the concept of forced labor. Frank Weston, the Anglican bishop of Zanzibar, was one of the most uncompromising critics, and his scathing attack on the Kenyan labor policies entitled *The Serfs of Great Britain* helped push the Colonial Office to order Northey to issue a new circular spelling out greater protections for African laborers.

The Kenyan authorities had better luck defending the Registration of Natives Ordinance, which required all African men and boys over the age of fifteen to carry a special labor passport, known as a *kipande* (piece, slip) in Swahili, that recorded their fingerprints, tribal origins, biographical data, and employment record. Carried in a metal case worn around the neck, the *kipande* was one of the great innovations in the history of empire. For once, an imperial power had a viable way to keep track of rural people, and the *kipande* made it much harder for individuals to resist or evade oppressive policies by blending into a nameless subject majority. Men traveling outside their reserves had to supply it to any policeman or district officer on demand, and the chief registrar of natives kept a duplicate copy of each certificate, thereby making it possible to identify a man by his fingerprints.

Most significant, the system kept wages down because workers could not find a new job unless their previous employer signed off on their *kipande*. The most abusive settlers kept their laborers in virtual bondage by refusing to do so. Men who broke their contracts faced legal sanction, and the government made it easy for employers to prosecute them with a "Complaint of Desertion of Registered Slave" form. The Kenyan authorities issued more than one million new registration certificates by the end of the 1920s and charged roughly ten thousand men per year with kipande violations. Those

pressure, land shortages, commercialized agriculture, and class for-mation were far more effective than the Northey circulars in forcing poorer Africans to work.

Many of these people, however, went to Nairobi, Mombasa, and corporate plantations instead of the white highlands. Unable to offer decent wages, the settlers had to court laborers by giving them per-mission to raise their own crops and cattle on the vast unused por-tions of their farms. Under Kenyan law, these were supposed to be contract workers, but by 1930 there were approximately 120,000 of these "squatters" permanently occupying 20 percent of the land in the highlands. Ironically, some were working land that had belonged to their families in the preconquest era. This squatter system was cheap but inefficient. Exploiting African peasant production was hardly a mark of progressive agricultural development, and the settler farm was more of a "feudal estate" than a capitalist enterprise.[41]

Seeking greater dignity and autonomy, some landless people understandably preferred "trespassing" in the native reserves of other tribes to squatting or working for Europeans. This illegal migration had the added benefit of providing an escape from chiefly supervision and taxation. In effect, it was a way to cease being a tribesman. For the Kikuyu, the nearby Maasai reserve was a tempting destination. Cov-ering almost fifteen thousand square miles of prime agricultural land, it had a population density of just three people per square mile. The approximately forty thousand Maasai held title to such a vast swath of territory by virtue of a pair of treaties with the IBEAC that were a legacy of their participation in the conquest of the highlands.[42] These treaties barred the Kenyan government from redrawing their tribal boundaries to relieve population pressure in the most overcrowded regions on either side of the Rift Valley. District officers were legally bound to send interlopers back to their reserves, where they had little chance of competing with the chiefs and mission school graduates who had already appropriated the best land.

Although they were the privileged elite of the reserves, these chiefly and educated intermediaries also disliked being treated like imperial subjects and bitterly resented the settlers' dominance of the white highlands. In 1925, a more aggressive younger generation of Kikuyu took control of Thuku's East Africa Association and trans-formed it into the Kikuyu Central Association (KCA). Although the chiefs tended to distrust the mission-educated men of the KCA,

who destroyed or tried to forge the certificates faced stiff fines and three months in jail.

Africans, understandably, detested the system. They found the fingerprinting demeaning and compared the metal kipande case and neck strap to a dog collar. Harry Thuku, a mission-educated telephone operator, fanned this widespread anger to organize the first mass African political resistance to imperial rule. Using popular discontent over wage cuts, high taxes, settler land seizures, and most particularly the kipande system as catalysts, he founded the East Africa Associa-tion (EAA) in 1921. The Association claimed to be nonpolitical, but it challenged the government's unqualified support for the settlers. Thuku audaciously held public meetings where women and girls recounted rapes on settler farms, and he called on people to turn in their kipandes en masse for delivery to the governor. The authori-ties found this sort of organized opposition intolerable. In 1922, the Kenyan police arrested Thuku for subversion and forcibly broke up a crowd that gathered to demand his release. In doing so they injured twenty-five and killed Mary Nyanjiru. By all accounts, she was of common origins, but her death and the mass protest forced the gov-ernment to reduce the poll tax from sixteen shillings to twelve and address some of the worst labor abuses. However, the imperial regime refused to acknowledge that it had bowed to African pressure, and it tried to cover up the riot and Mary Nyanjiru's death by exiling Thuku and shutting down his association.

Banning the EAA appeared to smother the kipande protests, but the Kenyan authorities did not understand that simmering tensions in the countryside were the greatest threat to British rule. By the 1920s, many of the twenty-four separate native reserves, which cov-ered more than forty-six thousand square miles, had become con-siderably overcrowded and eroded. With average population growth rates ranging from 1 to 2 percent per year, it was only a matter of time before they lost the capacity to support subsistence agriculture. Conditions were most severe in the three Kikuyu districts of Nyeri, Kiambu, and Fort Hall (Murang'a), where population densities of roughly 280 people per square mile forced up to three-quarters of the able-bodied men in some localities to leave home in search of work. The strain was almost as intense in the densely populated Luo and Luhya reserves in western Kenya, where between one-quarter and one-half of the adult men also became labor migrants.[40] Population

almost every Kikuyu shared a deep antipathy toward the reserve system. For this reason, many of the imperial regime's most important allies quietly backed the association's decision to send Jomo Kenyatta to London in 1929 to petition the British Parliament for relief from oppressive land and labor policies.

The metropolitan authorities refused to even consider the KCA's appeal on the technicality that it did not come through the Kenyan government. Nevertheless, pressure from the humanitarian lobby forced the Colonial Office to create a special commission to investigate Kenya's ethnically based land policies. Although British officials had no sympathy for the KCA, the environmental degradation of the North American dust bowl and rapid African population growth raised the prospect that the agricultural foundation of the tribal economies might collapse, thereby rendering the entire system of indirect rule unsustainable. The Kenya Land Commission's main concern was to protect the settlers' claim to the highlands by repairing the native reserve system. Its report ruled that the reserves were sufficient for the needs of Kenya's tribes, but it recommended an ambitious conservation and development program to increase the carrying capacity of African land. Acknowledging the growing African land hunger, the commissioners called only for a small revision of the tribal boundaries as well as opening some marginal parts of the forest reserves for African settlement.

In defending the racial and ethnic division of land in the colony, the Land Commission gave the government sanction to begin expelling surplus squatters from the highlands. While they needed some Africans to work their land, by the 1930s the settlers were growing increasingly anxious about the size of squatter families on their farms. Coming to the realization that the generation of Kikuyu growing up in their midst was essentially colonizing the white highlands, the Kenyan authorities began a program of forced relocation that sent tens of thousands people back to the already overcrowded reserves on the premise that improved soil conservation would open more land for them.

This entirely unrealistic assumption demonstrated the imperial regime's commitment to favoring the interests of the European minority over those of its African subjects. The settlers' entrenched privileges subjected the African population of Kenya to an unprecedentedly burdensome form of imperial subjecthood. Ancient

Britons, medieval Iberians, early modern Andeans and Bengalis, and perhaps even Napoleon's Italian subjects would have recognized the basic template of the new imperialism's extractive policies. Imperial tribute took many forms throughout history, but its ultimate origin was always subject labor. This remained the case in British Kenya. What was really new about the Kenyan experience of empire was the biologically determined racism of the new imperial regime. Although earlier empires were equally, if not more, violent, they did not see their subjects as fundamentally and irredeemably inferior. Romanization was an avenue to imperial citizenship, Iberians converted to Islam, and at least some Andeans and Bengalis stood a reasonable chance of blending into the imperial ruling class during the early modern era. Indeed, even Napoleon held out the possibility of assimilation through *amalgame*. In the modern era, however, Kenyans were permanently inferior and at the mercy of the politically connected settler class.

Few of the young Britons staffing the lowest levels of the imperial administration in the interwar era were willing to stand up to the settlers, but at least they believed in the new imperialism's civilizing rhetoric. Nevertheless, they still spent most of their time traveling about their districts collecting taxes, recruiting labor, and supervising the chiefs. Their superiors in Nairobi expected them to do little more than maintain law and order while keeping revenue flowing. Just as Napoleon measured his prefects by their ability to extract tribute, the Kenyan district officer's reputation turned on tax collection. Terence Gavaghan was frank in his recollection of the unpleasant realities of wringing wealth from a poor and marginalized peasantry. "In itself the extraction of cash, often at the cost of sale of small stock, from people in bare subsistence, was unedifying and burdensome. It was also a tedious and grubby task."[43] Gavaghan's Roman, Umayyad, Spanish, and Napoleonic peers would have agreed with these sentiments. Yet in the Kenyan case tax collection generated embarrassingly small returns, and the real mission of Gavaghan and his colleagues was to drive Africans into the labor market.

Under the principles of indirect rule, the day-to-day responsibility for imperial administration fell to the chiefs rather than district officers. While it is tempting to view the Kenyan chiefs as the equivalents of the Andean *kurakas*, Bengali *zamindars*, and other earlier imperial intermediaries, the "native authorities" in British Kenya had far less power than their predecessors. Some had influence before the conquest, but the vast majority were imperial functionaries who drew their status from the Kenyan state. Many were ambitious men who had made themselves useful to the IBEAC. Others were former enemies, such as Koitalel's oldest son, Lelimo, who made their peace with the new regime. But in all cases, the key qualification for being a chief was outward obedience and the ability to enforce imperial policy. Although they claimed that "native custom" was the basis of indirect rule, British officials often simply invented new traditions to justify investing their allies with chiefly authority. Thus, the Luhya paramount chief Mumia acquired a cloak with a grandly embroidered fringe and a silver-topped baton as symbols of his office. These trappings fooled no one, and ultimately the chief's day-to-day power rested on the tribal police force and, by extension, the imperial regime.

Like most imperial rulers, however, the Kenyan authorities were actually poor patrons, and it was quite difficult to be a tribal chief. The British expected their proxies to assist in tax collection, maintain order, produce labor, and stifle political opposition. These were unpopular measures, and the inherent weakness of the imperial state meant that "native authorities" needed at least some measure of local support to govern effectively. But the chief who tried to be too popular by protecting his constituents faced replacement. As a British official admitted: "Either they had to work in our interests and risk unpopularity which in their un-natural position was fatal to them, or they had to side with their people against us and thus become the instruments of their subjects while they pretended to help us. Most of them tried to do both and failed all around."[44]

Those who managed this difficult balancing act reaped considerable dividends. By the interwar era, the chiefs earned annual salaries of up to eighteen hundred shillings at a time when an unskilled laborer was lucky to make two hundred shillings in a year.[45] Moreover, the chiefs' control of the native courts and tribal police created ample opportunities for graft and corruption. They could also manipulate young district officers, who rarely developed a conversational command of African languages. The chiefs further dominated the local native councils that managed tribal finances in the most politically active reserves. As virtual tyrants in their locations, with the privilege of defining custom and tradition, they could punish rivals and claim

what was supposedly communal tribal land for themselves. Many Kikuyu chiefs used this land to grow cash crops and invested their earnings in businesses and education for their children.

The Kenyan government's insistence on treating Africans as primitive tribesmen legitimized and masked the chiefs' self-serving individualism. Assuming that African identities were exclusively collective, the imperial authorities would deal with Africans only as members of tribal communities. Common Africans understandably often found these designations limiting and oppressive, but the realities of the native reserve system meant that they had to accept their tribal status to gain access to land. The imperial authorities pretended that the reserves belonged collectively to the tribe and claimed that private land tenure was a western innovation with no precedent in native custom. In the 1920s, the Kenyan supreme court went so far as to rule officially that the Kikuyu in particular had no individual land rights. Arguing that privatization would create an exploitative landlord class, fragment the most productive land, and encourage social conflict, government officials repeatedly rejected petitions by wealthy Kikuyu for title deeds.

Profoundly suspicious of any practice or institution that might lead to "detribalization," the Kenyan government discouraged class formation and individualism. District officers and missionaries ridiculed Africans wearing western clothing, and the Education Department refused to let the mission schools teach in English on the grounds that, as one Colonial Office study put it, "tribal vernaculars" strengthened "the moral sanctions that rest on tribal membership."[46] In other words, peasant farmers did not need English, and European employers could use a simplified form of Swahili (popularly known as "ki-settler"), consisting largely of common objects and commands, to communicate with African workers. The Kenyan education authorities further mandated that government and mission schools teach an adapted curriculum that combined vocational training with tribal culture. They hoped that these measures would preserve the integrity of an imagined classless tribal society.

This imperial fiction was impractical and unsustainable given the social and economic realities of the new imperialism. The primary purpose of the native reserve system was to produce cheap African labor, not protect the viability of tribal society. The overcrowded Kikuyu reserves became particularly tense in the interwar era as family and clan members vied with each other to claim the most productive land. The stakes in these contests were high. Those who could control land and labor could produce lucrative cash crops for sale in nearby Nairobi or for export to the wider world via the railway. Although most of these entrepreneurs were Christians, their wealth enabled them to marry multiple wives. This meant that younger men, who could not afford to marry, faced the prospect of perpetual bachelorhood. Some worked for wealthy men, but the majority became labor migrants or squatters.

Those Africans who ventured outside their home reserves entered a world where Europeans enjoyed unquestioned preeminence and privilege. Asserting that there were no racial distinctions in Kenya, the imperial regime claimed that the Europeans' preeminence in the colony stemmed from their superior civilization rather than their race. This fatuous assertion allowed the settlers to use their control of the local legislative process to create a formidable system of racial discrimination and segregation. Not only did this "colour bar" make it illegal for Africans to live permanently in the cities and the highlands, it also followed the American model of social segregation by banning them from European hospitals, hotels, bars, schools, and churches. The settlers even rejected the Carnegie Foundation's offer to build a free library in Nairobi because it would have been open to Africans, albeit through a separate door.

The settlers' nearly total dependence on cheap and plentiful subject labor made the colour bar supremely hypocritical. Real segregation would have bankrupted them and destroyed the greatest perquisites of empire. In addition to tending the settlers' crops and building their cities and towns, Africans also looked after the settlers' personal whims. By the end of the 1930s, there were more than eight thousand African domestic servants in Nairobi alone. Under Kenyan law these butlers, cooks, nurses, and nannies were the only natives eligible for permanent residence in European areas, and most settler' houses included extensive servant quarters. Western children led such an exceedingly privileged life that the imperial authorities actually became concerned that the boys would lapse into sloth and degeneracy.

The settlers worried even more about how life in imperial Africa would affect their wives and daughters. Imagining that western women were the embodiment of civilization and virtue, they believed

that they needed constant protection, particularly from sexually rapacious native men. Most African household servants in Kenya were male, which meant they were a source of both domestic comfort and danger. Although they obsessed about this "black peril," the settlers would not give up the luxury of having Africans cook and clean for them. These gendered racial biases placed an enormous burden on western women to uphold the prestige of the settler class. Lord Cranworth cautioned that only the right kind of women who could learn when it was the "right time to have a servant beaten" should settle in Kenya, and any white woman caught in a voluntary "unlawful carnal connection with a native" faced up to five years in prison. Settler men were informally exempt from the ban on cross-cultural sex. Although the Colonial Office circulars banned conjugal relations with Africans, Terence Gavaghan's immediate superiors suggested that he take a mistress to help him polish his conversational Swahili. Too junior to attract the attention of a settler's daughter, he credited a series of African women with tutoring him in the "intricacies of sex."[47]

Gavaghan was free to indulge himself in the reserves, but Nairobi was supposed to be a safe and segregated bastion for European women. On paper, it was an exclusively white city, but this was never the case. In 1926 its population of roughly thirty thousand was approximately 60 percent African, 30 percent South Asian, and only 10 percent European. The vast majority of the African population lived in informal "villages" that the Nairobi municipal council refused to recognize as legitimate settlements. While these urban equivalents of rural "locations" in the reserves lacked even the most basic amenities, they offered refuge from taxation and the vagrancy laws that made it illegal for Africans to live permanently in the city. They were also good places to discuss politics, market produce from the reserves, and fence goods stolen from settler houses because they were largely outside the authority of the chiefs, district officers, and police. Crime was a problem in Nairobi from its earliest days, and in the 1920s African burglars had learned to break open safes, avoid leaving fingerprints, and escape in automobiles.

The municipal authorities therefore tried frantically to stamp out unauthorized African settlements and pulled down an average of thirty to forty illegal dwellings each week. But by the early 1920s, they had to accept the African "locations" of Pumwani and Kariokor (on the site of the old Carrier Corps depot) as permanent neighborhoods.

They could also do nothing about Kibera, a location that began as a settlement of discharged Sudanese veterans of the King's African Rifles. This did not, however, mean that they provided these African settlements with water, sewage, or other basic amenities.

The Nairobi municipal council justified this policy of malignant neglect on the grounds that Africans were temporary labor migrants who would eventually return to homes and families in the reserves. Apart from a small percentage of nurses and nannies, the logic of the colour bar also dictated that urban Africans were to be almost exclusively male. This freed employers from having to pay the higher wages needed to support a family in the city and allowed them to house their workers in simple barracks. The municipal authorities never could enforce these provisions, but their single-sex residence policies meant that the ratio of men to women in Nairobi was approximately eight to one by the end of the 1930s. The humanitarian lobby worried that this imbalance would lead to crime and vice, but more pragmatic government officials believed that a small number of prostitutes could tend to the migrants' needs.

The relatively few young African women who settled in Nairobi endured the indignities of urban imperial life because the cities provided an escape from the reserves, where the imperial regime rewarded the chiefs by backing their authority over tribeswomen. Some female migrants did work as prostitutes, but others provided rooms, home-brewed alcohol, and other basic domestic services. Although these arrangements made the government's gendered labor policies more bearable, the end result was a surge in rootless young people who swelled Nairobi's informal economy by the end of the interwar era. Worried that this "urban crowd" would follow political agitators like Harry Thuku, the municipal authorities finally admitted the necessity of allowing Africans to bring their families to the city.

The imperial regime's inability to keep the settled areas "white" exposed its inherent weakness. Illegal urban migration was just one of many strategies that Africans of all walks of life used to lessen the weight of the new imperialism. Lacking the means to resist openly, local communities took advantage of the Kenyan government's inability to govern them directly. A profusion of labor unrest and strikes in the late 1930s hinted at the potential of collective action, but in the interwar era vagrancy, trespassing, cattle rustling, prostitution, moonshining, and burglary were the most sensible and effective survival strategies for common people.

This was in contrast to the small handful of converts and mission school graduates whose mastery of western culture and English literacy qualified them for relatively lucrative careers as teachers, clerks, and interpreters. Free from the need to trespass in foreign reserves or live by their wits in the informal urban economy, they used the legitimizing ideologies of the Kenyan state. In founding their independent churches and schools, they sought to break the link between Christianity, western culture, and imperial authority by demonstrating that they too were a civilized people. The independent church movement first took hold among the Luo and Luhya communities before World War I and then spread to the Kikuyu reserves in the interwar period. Beginning with debates over the translation and interpretation of the Bible, independency rapidly became a moral and political force. Ultimately, the converts imagined a new African Christian society freed from the condescension of the missions and the political dominance of the settlers, but in the short term they wanted the freedom to conduct their own baptisms, marriages, and other religious rituals.

The Kikuyu independents in particular rejected Anglican and Presbyterian attacks on their culture and established a series of breakaway churches in the early 1920s. The confrontation came to a head in 1929 over the missionaries' insistence that their converts renounce female circumcision. Galvanized by Jomo Kenyatta's eloquent defense (if not reinterpretation) of Kikuyu tradition, large numbers of Kikuyu deserted the missions for these new churches. Many converts returned in time, but the independent churches remained viable. In the mid-1930s, church elders brought in an archbishop of the African Orthodox Church in South Africa named Daniel William Alexander to ordain their clergymen. The Kenyan police's Criminal Investigation Division kept the "coloured" Archbishop under surveillance, and the missions refused to recognize his baptisms and ordinations.

Despite these obstacles, Alexander's work legitimized the Kikuyu independent churches and, more important, their schools. In many ways, African demands for formal education lay at the root of the independence movement. At a time when schooling offered the best chance to escape the imperial regime's unyielding labor demands, African parents were immensely frustrated that the Kenyan government

era, the imperial lobby still promised to provide protected markets, new frontiers for settlement, and military manpower for the coming war. While some contemporary imperial sympathizers argue that the Colonial Office developed plans to train subject peoples for self-rule in the late 1930s, no one in official or unofficial imperial circles ever really imagined dismantling the empire at this point.

British officials optimistically believed that they could fix the imperial system to make it more acceptable to their subjects. On this score they were willing to grant non-Europeans a measure of self-government so long as they remained within the overall umbrella of the empire. In India, the first elections under the new Government of India Act gave the Indian National Congress control of India's provinces and most of its central administration in 1937. But loosening their hold on the Raj only made the British government more committed to retaining the rest of the empire. In 1938, the Colonial Office launched an ambitious new development initiative that promised to make good on the imperial lobby's grand promises about the mutual benefits of empire building. Its Colonial Development and Welfare Act of 1940 earmarked five million pounds per year for the development of "any colony or the welfare of its people." To a large degree, this was an answer to critics who equated the most oppressive and racist aspects of the new imperialism with Nazi fascism.

The realities of the Second World War postponed these development initiatives and forced Britain to instead make heavy demands on the empire. The wartime government implemented uncompromising extractive policies that wrung food, raw materials, manpower, and capital out of its remaining imperial territories around the world. Britain reasserted direct control over the Raj after the Indian National Congress withdrew from the government to protest its unilateral decision to draw India into the war with Germany. Putting aside the power-sharing compromises of the 1930s, British officials committed more than two million Indian men and 286.5 million pounds' worth of Indian goods to the imperial war effort and obligated the Raj to pay the operating costs of Indian Army units serving abroad. Common Indians paid the price for these contributions in the form of heavy manpower demands, higher taxes, and widespread food shortages.

By comparison, the war was a boon to the Kenyan settlers. Japanese conquests in the Far East eliminated much of their competition and the increased global demand for food and raw materials opened new

provided school spaces for only about thirty thousand of their children at the close of World War I.[48] This meant that just over 1 percent of the nearly three million Kenyan Africans had access to the "civilizing" western education that was a central ideological prop of the new imperialism. Even worse, there were only several hundred secondary school places for Africans.

This explains the school building boom in the Kikuyu reserves in the years before the Second World War. In 1936, the Education Department estimated that the independent institutions had enrollments of over five thousand students. Kenyan officials would have preferred to close them down, but they lacked the legal authority. While they probably could have an invented an excuse to do so, it would have been difficult to explain to the humanitarian lobby why teaching English, Christianity, and western values constituted an illegal act. At a time when modern communication gave the metropolitan government and general public the means to exercise unprecedented oversight over the wider empire, the imperial authorities had to appear to make good on their legitimizing rhetoric by giving their subjects at least some access to western culture and education.

The Kenyan government did not grasp the potential power of independence because its district officers still believed most Africans thought tribally and locally. The imperial authorities did not understand that discriminatory and oppressive land and labor policies and the inherent racism of the colour bar inspired Africans to imagine a larger, potentially violent, collective response to the imperial regime. In 1938, Jomo Kenyatta, the future president of Kenya, issued the prophetic warning that his fellow subjects were beginning to realize that it would take united action, if not force, to regain their freedom. Appropriating the imperial terminology of "the African," he cautioned that "he realises that he might fight unceasingly for his own complete emancipation; for without this he is doomed to remain the prey of rival imperialisms, which in every successive year will drive their fangs more deeply into his vitality and strength."[49]

Confident in their power, neither the metropolitan British government nor the Kenyan imperial regime paid much attention to Kenyatta's threat. Even as war with Germany loomed, most Britons still assumed that the empire would last for centuries. As Britain recovered from the depression, the African territories seemed particularly secure. Brushing aside the economic failures of the interwar

markets and drove up prices. In 1941, Kenya and the other East African territories assumed primary responsibility for supplying British forces during the North African campaign. Never before had Kenya's exports been so profitable, but these factors alone did not account for the European community's sudden prosperity. African farmers were still much better equipped to produce for the global market, and the settlers remained hamstrung by inefficiency and high labor and transport costs. Wartime emergency measures made the Colonial Office much less likely to intervene to protect African interests, which gave the Kenyan government the opportunity to expand subsidies and price supports for European agriculture. Settler leaders also maneuvered Kenyan officials into buying their maize at nearly twice the African rate on the grounds that peasant farmers had lower production costs and should be discouraged from overplanting to protect the soil. In practice, speculators bought African maize for resale at the higher European rate and manipulated mandatory livestock auctions in the reserves to do the same thing with African cattle.

The imperial special interests also secured cheap African labor by convincing the government to classify their enterprises as "essential undertakings." While this designation was supposed to apply only to strategically important sectors of the economy, the Kenya authorities broadened its definition to include the production of tea, coffee, and virtually anything else that could grow in the white highlands. The essential undertakings legislation also allowed the settlers to requisition conscripted civilian laborers. Pressure from metropolitan Britain forced the Kenyan government to revise these rules in 1943 to exclude some of the most embarrassing abuses, but not before the settlers made windfall profits. Conversely, although some African farmers also benefited from rising wartime prices, in 1943 food exports and a labor shortage brought on by civil conscription and military recruiting caused widespread famine in many reserves.

Britain paid a political price for asking so much of its subjects during the war. Although Winston Churchill insisted that the 1941 Atlantic Charter, which affirmed that all peoples had the right of national self-determination, applied only to Nazi-occupied Europe, British imperial subjects thought otherwise. Others concluded that an Axis victory was their best hope for emancipation, and some West Indian movie audiences cheered newsreels reporting Allied defeats. Similar sentiments prevailed in Asia, where more than thirty thousand

Indian prisoners of war and deserters fought for the Japanese in Subhas Chandra Bose's Indian National Army. In 1942 and 1943, India itself experienced the worst outbreak of violent opposition since the 1857 mutiny when anti-imperial groups attacked post offices, train stations, and other government installations. The Raj responded to Gandhi's even more damaging nonviolent Quit India movement by jailing him and the rest of the Indian National Congress leadership. There were no comparable outbreaks of violence in Kenya, but the government took no chances and jailed the leaders of the Kikuyu Central Association on the trumped-up charge of conspiring with the Italians in Ethiopia.

These draconian measures bought the empire time, but the British government recognized that it would have to give its subjects a stronger reason to support the Allied war effort. In 1942, Sir Stafford Cripps, the leader of the House of Commons, offered the Indians full dominion status or some alternative form of complete autonomy within the British Commonwealth, which suggested an empire of consent rather than coercion. One year later, the secretary of state for the colonies made a broader pledge to guide all "colonial peoples along the road to self-government within the framework of the British Empire."[50] Imperial officials tried to qualify and retreat from these statements after the war, but there was no denying that peace would bring significant change to the empire.

This was apparent even in metropolitan Britain, where the Labour Party's victory in the 1945 elections testified to a general weariness with the war and the expense of empire. The British public wanted rapid demobilization, jobs, heat, and housing, and most people were unwilling to expend precious resources on retaining India or any other imperial territory by force. While retreat from India would have been unthinkable in the interwar era, these sentiments reflected the reality that Britain no longer profited from the Raj. Metropolitan manufacturers had already lost their share of Indian markets, and wartime spending and borrowing meant that Britain actually owed India more than one billion pounds in 1946. Acknowledging these realities, British officials hoped to guide India's path to independence and shape its postimperial government. Instead, violent sectarian civil strife resulting from irreconcilable differences between the Hindu and Muslim communities forced Britain to withdraw its troops rapidly in 1947 and accept the partition of the Raj into India and Pakistan.

Most people in Britain recognized the necessity of Indian independence by this point, but the demise of the Raj gave imperial partisans an opening to make the case for retaining the rest of the empire. As Cold War tensions mounted, the Labour foreign secretary Ernest Bevin spoke of turning the remaining African and Asian territories into a "third force" as a global counterbalance to the United States and Soviet Union. More important, the economic problems of the postwar era gave the Labour government a powerful incentive to try once again to make the empire pay its promised dividends. Nearly six years of total war left the nation with a debt approaching three billion pounds just as the United States ended its lend-lease program. In what angry British officials termed a "financial Dunkirk," the American government forced Britain to ratify the Bretton Woods accord and eliminate its imperial trade barriers as a condition for further aid. Clement Attlee came to power on a platform of reconstruction, economic development, and social reform, but his government lacked the dollars to retire its debts and pay for imports of food and building materials. As a result, the British public faced greater shortages and deprivation in 1946 and 1947 than it had during the war years.

Many Britons therefore hoped that the imperial interests' promises about the value of the African territories might hold true. Several members of Attlee's government had been strong critics of the imperial excesses of the interwar years, but they believed that they could create a more humane and mutually beneficial system of imperial development now that they were in power. They assumed they could transform subject societies through central planning, mechanization, and the 120 million pounds that an enhanced Colonial Development and Welfare Act allocated for investment in the empire. Colonial secretary Arthur Creech Jones, a onetime Fabian socialist, spoke optimistically about raising living standards in the colonies, but the real purpose of postwar colonial development was to earn dollars for Britain.

To this end the Labour government initiated an ambitious program of development in Africa that was channeled largely through the new Colonial Development Corporation and other semiofficial enterprises. Blaming stunted African economies on the failure of free market capitalism, the Labourites believed that rational economic planning and state-sponsored investment could unlock the economic potential of the remaining empire. One of their biggest and most infamous projects was the sprawling Tanganyika groundnut scheme,

which spent thirty-six million pounds planting peanuts on tracts of land equal in size to the state of Connecticut. Similarly, a massive irrigation program in the Sudanese al-Jazirah province aimed to produce vast quantities of cotton. The overall goal of these initiatives was to provide raw materials that would reduce shortages in Britain and earn dollars in North American markets.

To this end, state marketing boards bought African produce at below-market prices on the promise that the banked surplus would guarantee stable returns in good times and bad. Rising global demand for commodities meant that there were no price downturns in the immediate postwar era, thereby allowing the territorial governments to keep the African deposits in London, where they were available for Britain's postwar recovery. The returns from African agriculture led the Colonial Office's development experts to meddle even more deeply in local communities. Failing to realize that African farmers were already willing and able to produce for the global market, their modernizing initiatives often alienated the very people they aimed to help.

The Labour development initiative also did very little to actually promote economic diversification or industrial development in Africa. In Kenya, the Colonial Development Corporation invested half a million pounds to turn a mix of improvised wartime industrial projects into East African Industries Ltd. (EAL), a semipublic conglomerate producing bricks, ceramics, tiles, chemicals, and cooking fats. These were money-losing ventures, and Asian investors and entrepreneurs had far more success in setting up small-scale industries that processed locally produced raw materials. None of these enterprises, however, altered Kenya's neomercantile relationship with Britain, and restrictive investment and licensing regulations ensured that commodity exports remained the central basis of the colony's economy.

From 1945 to 1951, Britain put forty million pounds into the empire, which was a fraction of the figure promised under the revised Colonial Development and Welfare Act. Nevertheless, the Labour government's various programs netted 140 million pounds for the metropolitan economy. This was in spite of debacles such as the Tanganyika groundnut scheme, which yielded only nine thousand tons of produce—meaning that a pound of its peanuts cost more than seventeen hundred pounds.[51] The resulting scandal almost brought down the Labour government.

Governor Mitchell shared this assumption. Seeking to lay the groundwork for a potential East African dominion, in 1946 he implemented a new legislative system that replaced his Executive Council with an "elected member system." This gave settler leaders control of key government departments, which evolved into formal ministries. Thus, Major Ferdinand Cavendish-Bentinck, the informal head of the postwar settler community, acquired the important portfolio for agriculture, animal husbandry and natural resources. By comparison, a former schoolteacher named Eliud Mathu became the sole appointed African representative in the lower Legislative Council until three more nominated African councilors joined him later in the decade.

On the surface, these measures appeared to make the Kenyan imperial regime more secure than ever. Population growth in the reserves ensured that employers had no difficulty recruiting African workers at comfortably low wages. Wartime profiteering gave the settler farmers the resources to invest in tractors and other forms of mechanization, which made them far less reliant on squatter labor. Able to dispense with the old imperial tools of labor extraction, they now sought to wall themselves off from all Africans but their domestic servants. Under settler pressure, sympathetic government officials resumed the mandatory relocations of the 1930s and forcibly returned roughly one hundred thousand squatters to the Kikuyu reserves between 1945 and 1952. These rural slums were no less crowded than they had been in the interwar era, but agricultural and social welfare experts hoped to develop them though soil conservation measures and modern agricultural technologies so that they could hold more people. This was entirely unrealistic, but it provided political cover for the Kenyan government's pro-settler policies.

The Labour government's mandate to end overt racism in the empire made this window dressing necessary. In 1948, the Colonial Office ordered the colonial governors to produce confidential memorandums justifying legislation in their territories that might be viewed as discriminatory. Mitchell's report was telling. While it boasted that Kenya had increased direct African representation on the Legislative Council, reformed the *kipande* system, and allowed lawful marriage between Africans and Europeans, it stoutly defended legal segregation in the colony on the basis of unequal "civilization." Arguing that the British government's earlier declarations in support of white settlement in Kenya amounted to a formal pledge

Most Africans, however, gave more than they got, and the Labourites' promises of mutual development proved ephemeral. As in the prewar era, British interests always came first. Metropolitan buyers had first call on building materials for reconstruction, and the African territories had to reduce consumption to keep their dollar earnings within the empire. These policies led to shortages, inflation, and greater state interference in the daily lives of African workers and farmers. The result was a wave of rural unrest and urban strikes that swept through British Africa in the postwar years. Most were over low wages and commodity prices, but the imperial authorities gradually recognized that they had the potential to mushroom into organized political resistance to British rule.

The Labour government's imperial experts naively believed that they could defuse this discontent by granting Africans a measure of local autonomy and reforming the most flagrantly abusive legal and social institutions. Certain that "the natives" were not ready for full independence, they promised to put their subjects on a gradual path to self-government. Creech Jones sought to replace indirect rule with a democratic system of local administration to bind educated Africans more closely to the imperial regime. Theoretically, qualified Africans would move from elected local bodies to seats on territorial legislative councils, which in time might become national parliaments as the colonies and protectorates evolved into autonomous entities within the Commonwealth. In the meantime, the Colonial Office directed district officers to be scrupulously courteous in their day-to-day dealings with African constituents and began to retire old Africa hands who, in the words of a new Colonial Service handbook, tended to like "primitive people but could not get on well with the educated native."52

Not surprisingly, none of these developments sat well with the Kenyan government or settlers. The old Africa hands remained firmly entrenched in the colony, and the postwar governor Sir Philip Mitchell believed that Kenya should develop along Rhodesian lines into a self-governing dominion. He consequently continued his predecessors' policies of encouraging additional settlement in the white highlands. As a result, migration spiked in the postwar era as a new generation of settlers swelled the European population of the colony to thirty thousand on the premise that it would continue to be a white man's country.

intrusive government regulations, and settler harassment were powerful incentives to think and act collectively. This became most evident in the strike that shut down the port of Mombasa in 1947 and a more serious general strike in Nairobi three years later. New African labor unions and the Kenya African Union (KAU), which began as an advisory body for African members of the Legislative Council, organized much of this opposition under Jomo Kenyatta's leadership.

The imperial authorities kept the KAU and the unions under close surveillance, but the independent Kikuyu churches, schools, and other less formal bodies were a more serious threat. In appearing to be apolitical and respectable, they provided cover for common people to discuss how to oppose oppressive imperial policies. Police informers reported that many had become radicalized, but the new postwar environment required the Kenyan government to prove that the independent congregations and schools had actually broken a law. With its capacity to rule authoritatively on the wane, the imperial regime used a network of spies and intelligence agents to monitor this opposition and relied on paramilitary police units and the King's African Rifles to cow potential rebels.

These were stopgap measures, and the Kenyan government's internal security systems failed entirely in the early 1950s when landless and unemployed young Kikuyu men fought back violently against the exploitation and injustices of British imperial rule. The bluff and intimidation that were the coercive linchpins of the new imperialism simply could no longer deter the enormous Kikuyu underclass, who had grown so desperate that they lost their fear of the imperial regime and its monopoly on lethal force. It is not clear when the Kikuyu squatters and slum dwellers first turned to violence, but the first indications that something was amiss appeared in the late 1940s, when the settlers started to notice hamstrung and mutilated cattle. The Kenyan authorities were slow to see the import of these developments, and they did not grasp the scope of the danger until the early 1950s, when the rebels assassinated the Kikuyu senior chief Waruhiu and massacred a handful of European families on remote farms. These murders threw the settlers into a panic, but as was the case with the Tupac Amaru revolt in the eighteenth-century Andean highlands, the guerrillas' primary targets were the elite members of their own community who appeared to prosper from cooperating with the imperial regime.

to the "European race," the governor insisted that any attempt to end the racial exclusivity of the highlands would be "regarded by all European inhabitants of the Colony as a serious breach of faith." Additionally, Mitchell maintained that laws requiring Africans to live in designated urban locations were not discriminatory because that was where they wished to live. He also claimed that vagrancy laws designed to prevent illegal migration to the cities primarily targeted "prostitutes and undesirables" and generally spared respectable people. Finally, and most hypocritically, he justified urban segregation as necessary to protect the health of the "non-native community" on the grounds that most Africans did not yet know how to follow the "elementary rules of hygiene."[53]

R. Mugo Gatheru, an inspector in the Public Health Department, agreed that conditions in the urban native locations were unsanitary, but he correctly laid the blame for this on the municipal authorities, which refused to provide African neighborhoods with water and other basic services. Citing a single public lavatory in Nairobi that was used by more than a thousand people and was little more than an irrigated trench, he offered this stomach-churning description of the consequences:

The water system was always defective and the faeces, therefore, could not be flushed away. Having no alternative, people would then continue "easing" themselves until the trench was full up. They would then be forced to use every inch of the floor until it became impossible to get inside—this became increasingly difficult to gauge since there were not enough lights within. The tins and floors were a sickening sight, and there were flies everywhere. One could see long threads or rings of tapeworms on the faeces dropped by people who were suffering from them, an inevitable disease amongst those forced to live in such circumstances.[54]

Mitchell justified segregation on the grounds that the more advanced European race made better productive use of Kenya's resources, but this public health disgrace and, by extension, the overall conditions in the slums and reserves were a more accurate record of the imperial regime's civilizing accomplishments.

These realities contributed directly to the increasing African unwillingness to tolerate imperial subjecthood in the postwar era. While their resistance tended to be local and relatively uncoordinated before the war, land shortages, rising prices, unemployment,

Operating from the cover of Nairobi slums and forested regions in the highlands, the rebels fielded a decentralized force of five thousand to six thousand men. Fighting in small bands, their primary weapons were homemade guns or firearms bought or stolen from the settlers and the army. A much larger group of civilian sympathizers supplied this armed faction with food and refuge. These people bound themselves to each other with a series of powerful oaths that had great weight in Kikuyu culture. The Kenyan authorities propagandistically depicted their vows as tribal, barbaric, and satanic, but in reality they were an effective means of countering the imperial regime's strategy of dividing the Kikuyu community. By the end of the conflict, it appears that almost every Kikuyu had taken at least one of these oaths, if for no other reason than to avoid retribution by the guerrillas. Only the most committed mission converts, senior chiefs, and government allies took the risky step of breaking openly with the rebellion.

The British referred to the guerrillas and their sympathizers as "Mau Mau," but the Kikuyu fighters called themselves the Kenya Land Freedom Army. The term *mau mau* had no actual meaning in any Kenyan language, but it allowed the imperial regime to further portray its opponents as barbaric tribesmen who turned to violence because they could not cope with the pressures of "modernity." In hindsight, the Mau Mau upheaval was actually a civil war waged between the imperial regime's enemies and allies in local Kikuyu communities throughout central Kenya. In this sense it resembled the 1809 mass outbreak of popular peasant violence that targeted Napoleon's local proxies in the mountain of northern Italy.

Tellingly, the Kenyan authorities were not much better at controlling the countryside than their Napoleonic predecessors had been. Lacking the ability to rule directly, they tried to tip the scales in favor of their Kikuyu allies by recruiting a Home Guard under the command of the chiefs to fight the rebels. They claimed that these units consisted of "loyalists" who rejected the barbarism of Mau Mau, but most guardsmen enlisted under duress and many were at least tacit supporters of the rebellion. Caught between these opposing forces, many common Kikuyu tried to remain neutral and joined the Home Guard or took an oath only when they had to. Most understandably wanted to avoid fighting their neighbors and kinsmen and hoped to escape the imperial regime's violent response to the uprising.

This was a sensible strategy. Caught off guard by the scope of the revolt, the Kenyan authorities declared a state of emergency, banned the Kenya African Union, and falsely convicted Jomo Kenyatta for being the sinister force behind the insurgency. They also had no option but to turn to the metropolitan government for aid because they did not trust their own African soldiers and policemen even though most were not Kikuyu. The British military had few resources to spare at a time when its forces were tied down in Korea, Malaya, and West Germany, but the entrenched communist insurgency in Malaya demonstrated that it was risky to take an anti-imperial revolt lightly. Winston Churchill, whose Conservative Party returned to power in 1951, had this in mind when he sent an entire British army brigade to Kenya one year later.

Taking over military operations in the colony, the regular army pursued an effective counterinsurgency strategy that isolated the forest fighters from the general population by encircling the regions where they operated. These tactics, particularly using starvation as a weapon, harked back to the pacification campaigns of the late nineteenth century. All told, the army's search-and-destroy operations killed approximately twenty thousand Kikuyu, many of whom were not necessarily armed combatants, and brought the military dimension of the Emergency to an end by 1956.

The Kenya Land Freedom Army lost for a number of reasons. Although modern Kenyan nationalism depicted the revolt as an inclusive popular uprising, most of Kenya's other communities refrained from taking an active role because they viewed it as a Kikuyu movement. In this sense, the imperial regime's tribal policies paid a dividend. Equally significant, the Kenyan government took the draconian step of incarcerating almost the entire Kikuyu population in a network of prison camps and strategic villages on the assumption that all Kikuyu were guilty until proven innocent. This hearkened back to Viceroy Don Francisco de Toledo's plan to force the entire subject population of the Andeans into regimented *reducciones*. In keeping with their own collectivist rhetoric, the Kenyan imperial authorities essentially indicted and convicted the entire Kikuyu "tribe." Only documented loyalists escaped the sweep that emptied the white highlands and urban areas of Kikuyu, and by 1955 there were roughly seventy thousand people in detention camps scattered around Kenya, with about one million more in new fortified villages.

The new imperialism's civilizing veneer required the Kenyan authorities to promise to "rehabilitate" these captive Kikuyu through a program of social welfare, manual labor, and invented tribal counteroaths to break Mau Mau's hold on their superstitious minds. This seemingly humane enterprise masked the naked brutality of the government's anti–Mau Mau operations. Although the guerrillas killed only thirty-two Europeans during the Emergency (more died in road accidents during the same period), the imperial regime responded to the revolt with a retributive fury that rivaled its predecessor's violent response to the 1857 Indian Mutiny. Facing the prospect of the mass tribal uprising that had long haunted their deepest fears, the settlers fought ferociously to defend their imperial and racial privileges. They exercised considerable control over the counterinsurgency and rehabilitation programs through the elected member system that gave them a dominant voice in the Executive and Legislative Councils. Additionally, their young men filled the ranks of the Kenya Police Reserve, the all-white Kenya Regiment, the detention camp staffs, and much of the KAR's officer corps. This gave them the means to terrorize the Kikuyu population through murder, beatings, rape, physical mutilation, and torture.[55]

The Kenyan authorities covered up the vast majority of these incidents and excused those that came to light as a natural consequence of the public outrage over the slaughter of settler families. This was a fraud for the government itself was also deeply involved in the abuses. The Kenyan police frequently tortured confessions out of Kikuyu suspects, and state witnesses openly perjured themselves at trials that sent more than one thousand convicted Mau Mau members and supporters to the gallows.[56] Taken with Jomo Kenyatta's sham trial, these cases made a mockery of the British legal tradition that was supposedly one of the imperial regime's civilizing gifts to the subject peoples of the empire.

In time, reports of these abuses appeared in the metropolitan press, thereby shaming the British government and undermining public support for the imperial regime. Galvanized by the events in Kenya, an anti-imperial humanitarian lobby of liberally minded members of Parliament, socialists, and evangelicals came together to call for an end to settler colonialism throughout the empire. To a large degree their criticisms echoed the popular revulsion over the behavior of the nabobs in Bengal nearly three centuries earlier, but

the realities of the post–World War II era made the Kenyan imperial abuses far more embarrassing and unsustainable. It was impossible to reconcile the reports of torture coming out of East Africa with Article Seventy-six of the United Nations Charter, which committed Britain to putting its imperial subjects on the path "toward self-government or independence." Britain's record on this score became even more awkward as more and more former imperial territories joined the General Assembly and British Commonwealth as member nations after gaining their independence.

The metropolitan public found little reason to excuse the damage that the Kenyan fiasco did to Britain's national reputation, particularly after it became obvious that the new imperialism's promised returns were ephemeral. India, one of the last vestiges of the first British Empire, had been unquestionably profitable, but now it was gone. While exports from the remaining imperial territories helped generate dollar earnings after the war, the key factors in Britain's recovery were a grant from the Marshall Plan and the devaluation of the pound. By the mid-1950s, the wider empire bought just 13 percent of Britain's exports and supplied only 10 percent of its imports. Most territories ran up their own dollar deficits, which meant that they no longer played a role in supporting the pound.[57] With the empire becoming more of an obvious burden, many Britons began to ask whether they would be better served by joining the European Common Market than by wasting economic, diplomatic, and military resources trying to hold together the last vestiges of the empire.

Recognizing these realities, the Conservative governments of the 1950s adopted a pragmatic strategy of granting individual territories self-rule, followed by independence, on the condition that the new rulers respected British investments and remained within the western sphere of influence. Essentially, they sought to turn the clock back a century to revive the institutions of informal empire. Senior Colonial Office officials and later generations of imperial apologists tried to portray this retreat as part of a planned strategy, but their revisionism was really just an attempt to put the best face on events that had spun out of control. Moreover, the fiction of planned decolonization was plausible only in the Caribbean and West Africa, where there were no significant British expatriate populations. African majority rule in the settler-dominated territories in eastern and southern

Africa was a nonstarter because the British government had theoretically pledged that they would remain white.

In Kenya, the expense and international embarrassment of Mau Mau led metropolitan British officials to make limited concessions to buy time and win over moderate African leaders. Over the vehement objections of the settlers, who refused to share power under any terms, they offered non-Europeans a political role through constitutional "multiracialism." Continuing the imperial policy of granting rights to communities rather than individuals, multiracialism denied Africans a full vote on the grounds that they were not sufficiently advanced to qualify for the franchise. Contending that civilization was the basis of political representation, the Colonial Office drew up constitutions that granted voting rights only to propertied or educated Africans and allocated legislative seats based on disproportionate ethnic quotas. This ensured that Europeans outnumbered African representatives by a ratio of two to one.

The vast majority of Africans understandably detested multiracialism, and in 1957 most African legislative council members boycotted the first elections held under the new constitution. Despite this opposition, the Kenyan authorities believed that they could water down this resistance. Sensing that popular opposition to multiracialism was breaking down tribal boundaries, they looked to divide the subject majority on the basis of class. To this end, they endeavored to create a small cadre of landed elites through a radical policy shift that gave their allies, particularly the Kikuyu chiefs and loyalists, the means to acquire private land titles in the reserves. Theoretically these prosperous commercial farmers would have a vested interest in supporting continued British rule in Kenya. In finally backing African agricultural development, the imperial planners hoped that the resulting surplus would drive industrial development, thereby reducing unemployment and relieving the colony's chronic land shortage, Hard-core settlers opposed these reforms to the very end, but more pragmatic government officials realized the colour bar was politically unsustainable. Buoyed by an entirely unrealistic War Office plan to develop Kenya into a major military base in the late 1950s, they hoped to win enough African support to push back the day when they might have to enfranchise the subject majority.

The metropolitan authorities did not actually have an explicit plan to abandon the empire at this point, and it is possible that British rule in Africa might have lasted longer had it not been for the 1956 Suez crisis. The United States' opposition to the British, French, and Israeli plot to undo Gamal Abdel Nasser's nationalization of the canal by reoccupying the Canal Zone under the guise of a peacekeeping mission was a powerful demonstration that the new imperialism was unsustainable in the Cold War era. Fearing that the Soviets would exploit the nonwestern world's near universal hostility to the Franco-British invasion, the American government forced Britain to withdraw by threatening not to support its application for a loan from the International Monetary Fund.

This humiliation drove Prime Minister Anthony Eden from office and brought Harold Macmillan to power. At a time when the French and Belgians were making plans to leave Africa and a new United Nations resolution called for full independence for subject peoples, Macmillan resolved that Britain would not be the last imperial power on the continent. To this end he told the South African parliament in 1960: "The wind of change is blowing through this continent, and, whether we like it or not, this growth of national consciousness is a political fact."[58] This declaration of Britain's intention to retreat from Africa was also a tacit admission that multiracialism had failed to blunt African demands for full citizenship, if not total independence. The Afrikaners were entirely unmoved by Macmillan's warning about the power of African nationalism and calculated that violent repression would keep them in power. Startled imperial officials in the rest of British Africa, however, found that true national independence was no longer a vague promise but an immediate reality.

In Kenya, the settlers complained indignantly that Macmillan had betrayed them, but they were swiftly losing their remaining support in metropolitan Britain. It cost the British taxpayer roughly fifty-five million pounds to rescue them from the Mau Mau uprising, and reports that jailors at the Hola detention camp had beaten at least ten Kikuyu prisoners to death touched off a public scandal that threatened Macmillan's majority in Parliament. Although the Conservative Party had a history of defending the empire, the Tories were now unwilling to risk their party's larger political fortunes by defending a privileged imperial elite. As one of the new younger generation of Conservative politicians told the settler leader Michael Blundell: "What do I care about the fucking settlers, let them bloody well look after themselves."[59]

Thus the wind of change swept through Kenya along with the rest of British Africa. Accepting that independence would come within a matter of years instead of decades, the Kenyan authorities hoped to turn over power to a friendly African regime that would respect British investment and guarantee the settlers' lives and property. At first they tried to accomplish this by allying with the leaders of the Kenya African Democratic Union's (KADU) minority communities. Sharing fears of domination by the more numerous Kikuyu and Luo peoples that constituted the Kenya African National Union (KANU), KADU cooperated with the British government in drafting a federal constitution that divided the new nation into seven autonomous tribally based regions under a weak central government. This would have meant that the settlers would have become simply another minority tribe with a constitutional guarantee of autonomy in the postimperial era. However, KADU won only 20 percent of the vote in the 1961 elections that chose a provisional government to guide Kenya to independence.

Although the settlers reviled him as the satanic force behind Mau Mau, Jomo Kenyatta proved to be the imperial regime's most useful African ally during this transitional period. Far from being a radical or socialist, as his critics suggested, he actually had closer ties through marriage and sentiment to the landed Kikuyu elite. He was also unquestionably innocent of the government's fabricated charges that sent him into detention and internal exile for almost a decade. but this inequity had the silver lining of sparing him from having to take sides during the Mau Mau civil war and established his credentials as a national hero. In August 1961, the authorities gave into the inevitable and released him. Although he claimed to be above politics, he won a landslide victory in the 1963 independence elections as the KANU candidate.

One of Kenyatta's first priorities on taking power on December 12, 1963, was to abolish the federal system, but in almost every other regard he proved surprisingly cooperative in working with his former imperial rulers. Declaring that all Kenyans had fought for independence, he passed over the former forest fighters and Mau Mau detainees in favor of influential ex-chiefs and loyalists when forming his new government. He made it clear that there would be no radical redistribution of land or wealth, committing Kenya to a program of capitalist development and emphasizing economic continuity and

respect for private property. Most important from the settlers' perspective, Kenyatta agreed to buy at above-market rates the land of any farmer who wanted to sell and to welcome those who wanted to stay. Although international donors provided the means for some common people to acquire a share of the former white highlands, most of the former settler farms went to the president's wealthy allies.

Many of the supporters who had hailed Kenyatta as a champion of the poor and landless during the imperial era were terribly disappointed by these policies. They assumed that *uhuru* (freedom) would bring land by breaking up the great highland farms and create jobs by forcing Europeans and Asians to leave Kenya. Yet the neomercantilist economy that the postimperial government inherited from the former regime largely tied Kenyatta's hands. Admittedly, his first priority was to secure his own power base by rewarding his closest allies, but the new president had few resources to make good on the promises of independence. After the transfer of power, the emptiness of the new imperialists' avowed commitment to civilize and modernize Kenya became painfully clear as Kenyatta's government strove to turn an artificial imperial conglomeration into a viable nation-state. The legacy of the colour bar and the dismally inadequate imperial education system meant that there were only a handful of Africans with the skills to guide Kenya through this transitional period. The new nation similarly inherited the imperial regime's narrow industrial base, inadequate infrastructure, and bleak urban slums. These were the new British Empire's true legacies.

The rapid and largely unexpected demise of the imperial regime in Kenya reflected the unstable and contradictory nature of the new imperialism. While the emergence of powerful national identities in the nineteenth century suggested there would be no more empires in Europe, western technological and capitalist advances appeared to give empire building a new lease on life in regions in Africa and Asia where identities remained dangerously local. Westerners took their short-term political, economic, and military advantages over these communities as evidence of their own cultural superiority, but the quick and relatively easy victories that built the new empires were simply the result of the uneven advance of globalization around the world. A broader historical view, coupled with the economic rise of the nonwestern world in recent years, reveals the fallacy of the racial and cultural chauvinism that legitimized the new imperialism.

What was actually novel about the new imperial projects was that largely democratic liberal nation-states were their sponsors. The voting western European public considered themselves civilized and moral and would not tolerate a return to the excesses of earlier imperial eras. Consequently, the new imperialists had to disguise their base ambitions by promising to create humane liberal empires that would reform and uplift subject societies in addition to bringing wealth and national glory to the imperial metropole. This intrinsic hypocrisy, which required empire builders to denigrate their Africans and Asians so they could save them, was also an innovative feature of the new imperialism. Early generations of empire builders were equally certain of their cultural superiority, but they never really pretended that their conquests were for the good of their subjects. No one in early modern Spain really took the rhetoric of the conquistadors' *requerimiento* seriously. Even more troubling, the rigidity of romanization or *amalgame* in the new imperialism.

The Kenyan imperial state was one of most oppressive manifestations of the new imperialism. It grafted its deceitful legitimizing ideologies onto a highly exploitive model of the kind of old-style settler colonialism that destroyed the Amerindian and Aboriginal civilizations of North America and Australia. Dressing the East Africa Protectorate's pacification campaigns in the garb of liberal humanitarianism was bad enough, but the settlers' argument that they were civilizing the peoples of the highlands by exploiting their labor was simply disgusting. As one dubious official in the Colonial Office acidly noted: "Does anyone really believe in the educative value of labour on a European farm?"[60] The reality of the settlers' self-avowed goal of making Kenya into a "white man's" country turned Africans into a permanent underclass. To be sure, ancient Britons, medieval Iberians, and early modern Andeans and Bengalis faced a similar fate, but at least their imperial rulers made no attempt to disguise their extractive agenda.

In the end, the African territories paid some of the worst returns in the history of empire. Although the native reserve system ultimately proved effective in forcing Africans to accept extremely low wages, inexpensive unskilled labor was not worth very much in the modern industrial era. At best, coerced African labor helped the settlers compensate for their lack of capital, high transportation costs, and basic agricultural incompetence, but it was not a basis for sustainable

development or even old fashioned imperial extraction. These economic realities were fairly typical of most new imperial territories.

It is therefore hardly surprising that the new empires of the late nineteenth century proved so ephemeral. Lasting less than a century, they were almost as short-lived as the aborted Napoleonic empire. The new British Empire in Africa that Frederick Lugard assumed would last for centuries fell apart once Africans acquired the means to mount an effective resistance by developing larger collective, if not protonational, identities based on the common experience of abuse and a mutual hatred of the imperial regime. In explaining the ultimate collapse of the Kenyan imperial state, Michael Blundell candidly admitted: "It boiled down to whether the British Government could or would shoot Africans to maintain the status quo for Europeans."[61] Earlier generations of empire builders would have unflinchingly obliged the settlers by killing people, but the Kenyan imperial regime had to at least make a show of living up to its humanitarian obligations.

Even more fundamentally, the metropolitan British government was bound by the new imperialism's legitimizing ideologies. Seeking to defuse African and Indian nationalism in the post–World War II era, the Labour government assured subject peoples that they were full and equal citizens of the empire. Its 1948 Nationality Act put this promise into law and opened the way for first tens and then hundreds of thousands of West Indians and South Asians to take the low-paying menial jobs that were vital to Britain's postwar reconstruction. Many stayed on to enjoy the higher standards of living in the imperial metropole. Never imagining that empire building would have such a profound impact on their own politics and culture, xenophobic Britons responded with race riots in the 1950s and a series of discriminatory immigration laws that gradually closed the door to non-European members of the Commonwealth a decade later.

There is no such thing as a liberal empire. The "new" British Empire in Africa fell quickly once Africans acquired the means to expose its inherent weaknesses. Like all empire builders, the architects of British Africa grossly underestimated their subjects. In Europe, however, another band of conquerors once again plunged the continent into tragedy and chaos by making the same mistake. Few historians see Adolf Hitler as product of the new imperial era, but his genocidal attempt to create a continental empire took the logic of the new imperialism to its bloody but inevitable conclusion.